The Campus History Series

BEAVER COLLEGE AND ARCADIA UNIVERSITY

Presented here are the Beaver Female Seminary and Arcadia University seals from 1853 and the present day. Female seminaries were private educational institutions for women. They were especially popular in the United States during the 19th and early 20th centuries, when opportunities in educational institutions for women were scarce. In the early 19th century, the word "seminary" began to replace the word "academy." The movement was a significant part of the transformation in American education from 1820 to 1860. Some of the seminaries gradually developed into four-year colleges, as was the case for the Beaver Female Seminary. (Beaver Female Seminary seal courtesy of Beaver Area Heritage Foundation Museum; Arcadia University seal courtesy of Arcadia University Archives.)

ON THE COVER: This photograph, maintained in the Arcadia University Archives, is documented with the year 1963 on the reverse side. It shows two students standing in one of the former five entrances/exits of the Harrison Estate located on the Easton Road/Limekiln Pike side of the property (in front of where Kistler Hall is located today). A Philadelphia Rapid Transit bus is seen in the background traveling northbound on Easton Road. (Arcadia University Archives.)

COVER BACKGROUND: This north view of Grey Towers was taken shortly after Beaver College's purchase of the Glenside property in 1929. (Arcadia University Archives.)

The Campus History Series

BEAVER COLLEGE AND ARCADIA UNIVERSITY

KENNETH SAMEN
INTRODUCTION BY DR. AJAY NAIR

ARCADIA
PUBLISHING

Copyright © 2024 by Kenneth Samen
ISBN 978-1-4671-6153-4

Published by Arcadia Publishing
Charleston, South Carolina

Printed in the United States of America

Library of Congress Control Number: 2024933730

For all general information, please contact Arcadia Publishing:
Telephone 843-853-2070
Fax 843-853-0044
E-mail sales@arcadiapublishing.com

Visit us on the Internet at www.arcadiapublishing.com

I dedicate this book to my wife, Melissa (Martin) Samen, class of 1993. In October 2023, we celebrated our 30th wedding anniversary. Pictured are Melissa and me in the Rose Room of the castle at the February 9, 1991, Castle Cotillion. Completing and gifting this book is the least I can do to thank Beaver College/ Arcadia University for the life I have been able to live by meeting my wife and for the degree that I earned.

—Kenneth Samen, class of 1992

CONTENTS

ACKNOWLEDGMENTS

Beaver College/Arcadia University's students, faculty, and alumni genuinely care about the university as an institution and as an extended family. Although the campus may look different due to the growth of the university, it still feels like home. Our individual time on the campus may have differed due to circumstances outside of the stone walls, such as war and conflict, social unrest, civil rights, and pandemics, but we still can come back where we will always be welcome. Documenting memories of the Glenside campus is essential for those who will attend, graduate from, and lead the university in the future. My hope is that the 35,000-plus Beaver College/Arcadia University alumni will enjoy this book and will want to come home. All author's proceeds from this book go directly to the university. The university's history has been well documented, even as recent as 2003 with the publishing of *A 150 Year History of Beaver College and Arcadia University* by Samuel M. Cameron, Mark Curchack, and Michael L. Berger. This publication is intended to be a supplement to prior documented histories, telling the story of how we got to where we are today via historical photographs. I wish to extend my sincere thanks and appreciation to all the contributors and lenders of photographs, historical memorabilia, and time (see each image for credit); without this effort, the book would not have been possible. Note, all photographs credited to "Arcadia University Archives" are all rights reserved and reprinted with permission of Arcadia University. Images may not be reproduced in any form, including in print or by any electronic means, without prior written permission from Arcadia University. I wish to extend my sincere thanks and appreciation to Melissa Samen; from Arcadia University: Anastasia Rousseau, project archivist; Matthew Borgen, exhibitions coordinator; Thomas Macchi, associate vice president for facilities management; Dan DiPrinzio, interim vice president of marketing and communications; Emily Horowitz, assistant director, marketing and communications; Margo Maas, associate director of young alumni and student engagement; Nicole Steiner, associate vice president for alumni engagement and annual giving strategies; Sarah Middleton, senior counsel; Margaret Callahan, general counsel and secretary; Brigette Bryant, vice president of development and alumni engagement; and Dr. Ajay Nair, president; as well as from Arcadia Publishing: Caitrin Cunningham, senior title manager, Katy Perry, associate publisher, and Mike Litchfield, senior production editor.

INTRODUCTION

It was 2017 when I first met with Arcadia University community members and the presidential search committee to discuss the possibility of serving as president of Arcadia University. What struck me most about this community was its welcome of authenticity. As president, Arcadia would allow me to embrace my own authenticity. I could be myself.

That tenet can be traced back more than 170 years to this institution's founding. In the mid-19th century, Beaver Female Seminary provided young women with a higher education at a time when such opportunities were significantly limited. Women were permitted to think big, prepare for future careers, and flourish as individuals.

In the pages that follow, you will see how a small female seminary evolved into a global coeducational university. While there have been many changes over the years to academic programs, the student body, and our expanding institutional footprint, all of our changes have been designed to provide the best possible educational experience. As we have worked to meet the needs of students throughout the years, what has remained constant through every iteration of this fine institution—from Beaver Female Seminary, to Beaver College and Musical Institute, to Beaver College, and now as Arcadia University—is sustaining a focus on fostering individuality and preparing students for success.

During my presidential tenure, we have built on the pioneering and trailblazing spirit of our earliest students and graduates to address the most pressing issues affecting our community. Our work has been challenging, but we eagerly accept the mantle and obligation to advance the strength and courage that the early administrators of this institution had in its formative years.

Today, Arcadia University is proud to count its thousands of students at our Glenside, Pennsylvania, and Christiana, Delaware, campuses, as well as thousands of students at our centers around the world. As of this writing, our alumni base is nearly 37,000 strong, each of whom carries the pioneering spirit of two women—Sylvania Jones and Juliette A. Poundstone—who started it all.

I hope all who read this book will see the Beaver College/Arcadia University legacy reflected through this storied history. This always has been and will remain a special place composed of extraordinary people. Thank you to Kenneth Samen for recognizing the value of sharing our history with the world and for asking me to be a small part of it.

—Ajay Nair, PhD
President, Arcadia University

Dr. Ajay Nair is a nationally recognized expert in student affairs issues and is an accomplished social justice, race, and ethnicity scholar. He was appointed the 22nd president of Arcadia University in April 2018 and inaugurated on October 13, 2018. Dr. Nair is the first person of color to be appointed president at Arcadia and is among the first college or university presidents of Indian American descent in the United States. Before joining Arcadia, Dr. Nair served in executive leadership positions at the University of Pennsylvania, Columbia University, and the University of Virginia. In his distinguished career in higher education, Dr. Nair has held faculty positions at each of the above universities, as well as at the World Language Institute in Kwangju, South Korea. (Arcadia University Archives.)

High-Level Timeline

Pittsburgh-area newspapers first mentioned Beaver Female Seminary due to its application for a charter of incorporation in late 1853. "In the Court of Common Pleas of Beaver County, No. 125, September Term, 1853. Application of Rev. Joshua Monroe and others, stockholders in said 'Beaver Female Seminary,' for a charter. And now, to wit, Sep. 13, 1853, The Court having perused and examined the same, and the objects, articles and constitution therein set forth and contained, appearing to the court lawful and not injurious to the community, order and direct the same to be filed in the office of the Prothonotary of this court, and that notice be given by the Prothonotary, inserted in the *Beaver Argus*, printed at the seat of justice, for at least three weeks before the next term, setting forth the application made to the court to grant their charter. Notice is therefore, hereby given, that unless cause against the same be shown on or before the first day of next term, if any cause there be, said charter will be granted by the court. John Collins, Pro. October 19, 1853."

1853: Beaver Female Seminary organizes in Beaver, Pennsylvania
1860: School name changes to Beaver Seminary and Institute
1865: School name changes to Beaver Seminary and Music Institute
1872: School name changes to Beaver College and Musical Institute, male students are admitted, and school becomes coeducational for the first time
1881: William Welsh Harrison Sr. purchases the Rosedale Hall Estate (38 acres) in Glenside, Pennsylvania
1893–1898: Harrison constructs Grey Towers in Glenside, Pennsylvania
1896: Pittsburgh Female College merges with Beaver College in Beaver, Pennsylvania
1907: School name changes to Beaver College; enrollment is again limited to women
1925: Beaver College merges with Beechwood College and relocates to Jenkintown, Pennsylvania
1928: Beaver College purchases 26 acres of the Harrison property in Glenside, Pennsylvania, from his estate (both the Jenkintown and Glenside campuses are used in unison)
1962: The former Glenside, Pennsylvania, property becomes Beaver College's single campus
1973: Male students are admitted and school becomes coeducational for the second time
1985: Grey Towers is designated a national historic landmark
2001: Beaver College obtains university status and the name is changed to Arcadia University

LIST OF PRESIDENTS

22 presidents (plus 5 acting):

Rev. Dr. Sheridan Baker (1855–1858)
Prof. Samuel Davenport (1858–1859)
Rev. Dr. Riley Treadway Taylor (1859–1894)
Prof. William J. Alexander (1894–1896)
Dr. Nicholas H. Holmes (1896–1898)
Dr. Arthur Staples (1898–1907)
Dr. George D. Cressman (1907–1909)
Dr. William W. Foster (1909–1910)
Dr. LeRoy Weller (1910–1917)
Dr. Horace Haskell (1917–1919)
Dr. C. Mase Thomas (1919–1921)
Dr. James M. Thoburn Jr. (1921–1923)
Dr. Lynn H. Harris (1923–1927)
Dr. Jesse Penney Martin (acting 1927–1928)
Dr. Walter Burton Greenway (1928–1939)
Dr. James E. Mooney (acting 1939–1940)
Dr. Raymon Kistler (1940–1960)
Dr. Edward Dwight Gates (1960–1983)
Dr. Bette E. Landman (acting 1983)
Dr. Bruce Wilson (1983–1985)
Dr. Bette E. Landman (1985–2004)
Dr. Jerry M. Greiner (2004–2011)
Dr. James P. Gallagher (acting 2011)
Carl "Tobey" Oxholm III (2011–2013)
Dr. Nicolette Deville Christensen (2013–2017)
George Hanks "Hank" Brown (acting 2017–2018)
Dr. Ajay Nair (2018–present)

One

1853–1928

BEAVER FEMALE SEMINARY TO BEAVER COLLEGE BEFORE PURCHASE OF GLENSIDE CAMPUS

Where the Ohio and Beaver Rivers meet in the westernmost part of Pennsylvania, the French established a trading post where members of the Delaware, Shawnee, and Iroquois tribes bartered with the European traders. The rivers were essential for travel, nourishment, and military defense. Gen. Lachlan McIntosh of Washington's Colonial Army built a fort in this location during the Revolutionary War. After the war, the fort was the home of the 1st American Regiment, the oldest active unit in the US Army. The fort was abandoned in 1788 and razed a short time later. In 1802, as the area's population expanded, the town of Beaver, Pennsylvania, was incorporated. Rev. Mathew Simpson, a bishop of the Methodist Episcopal Church, in conversation with the Reverend Joshua Moore, proposed the idea of a high school for young ladies to be established in the borough of Beaver, Pennsylvania. This quiet town was chosen because of its accessibility to the Ohio valley, its healthful atmosphere, and the "high moral and intellectual tone of its inhabitants." Monroe set out to gain the support of the citizens of Beaver. When he approached Daniel Agnew (later president of the board of trustees and chief justice of the state), he recommended that the new institution not be merely a high school but a seminary with chartered rights. The idea was enthusiastically accepted, and on December 28, 1853, the Beaver Female Seminary was founded. Life was strict for the students at the seminary in the early days. Students were not allowed off the school's property without permission and a chaperone. Students were only allowed to move about the grounds unchaperoned during the daytime. No visitors were allowed in private rooms, and rooms were inspected regularly. The lights were officially off at 10:00 p.m. via a main switch.

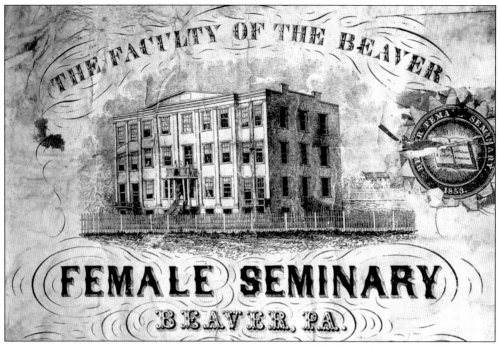

On December 28, 1853, the institution known today as Arcadia University was first organized as the Beaver Female Seminary. A sum of $3,500 ($138,950 in 2024) was raised for startup costs, including a building. Pictured is the 46-by-74-foot brick school building. It was three stories in addition to an attic and an above-ground basement. It housed a kitchen, laundry, dining room, and student housing and was completed by the fall of 1855. (Arcadia University Archives.)

The school was advertised as a "Seminary of learning for the education of female youths in the Art, Science and useful literature." Rev. Dr. Sheridan Baker (November 8, 1824–March 30, 1890, pictured here) was the first principal/president of the seminary, elected on April 3, 1856. Prior to his time at the Beaver Female Seminary, he was president of the Brownsville Female Seminary (established on April 14, 1838), located in Brownsville, Fayette County, Pennsylvania. (Arcadia University Archives.)

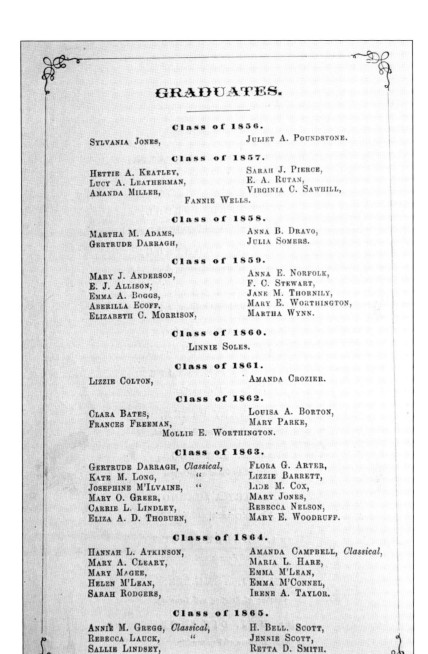

GRADUATES.

Class of 1856.

SYLVANIA JONES,
JULIET A. POUNDSTONE.

Class of 1857.

HETTIE A. KEATLEY,
LUCY A. LEATHERMAN,
AMANDA MILLER,
SARAH J. PIERCE,
E. A. RUTAN,
VIRGINIA C. SAWHILL,
FANNIE WELLS.

Class of 1858.

MARTHA M. ADAMS,
GERTRUDE DARRAGH,
ANNA B. DRAVO,
JULIA SOMERS.

Class of 1859.

MARY J. ANDERSON,
E. J. ALLISON,
EMMA A. BOGGS,
ABERILLA ECOFF,
ELIZABETH C. MORRISON,
ANNA E. NORFOLK,
F. C. STEWART,
JANE M. THORNILY,
MARY E. WORTHINGTON,
MARTHA WYNN.

Class of 1860.

LINNIE SOLES.

Class of 1861.

LIZZIE COLTON,
AMANDA CROZIER.

Class of 1862.

CLARA BATES,
FRANCES FREEMAN,
LOUISA A. BORTON,
MARY PARKE,
MOLLIE E. WORTHINGTON.

Class of 1863.

GERTRUDE DARRAGH, *Classical,*
KATE M. LONG,   "
JOSEPHINE M'ILVAINE, "
MARY O. GREER,
CARRIE L. LINDLEY,
ELIZA A. D. THOBURN,
FLORA G. ARTER,
LIZZIE BARRETT,
LIDE M. COX,
MARY JONES,
REBECCA NELSON,
MARY E. WOODRUFF.

Class of 1864.

HANNAH L. ATKINSON,
MARY A. CLEARY,
MARY MAGEE,
HELEN M'LEAN,
SARAH RODGERS,
AMANDA CAMPBELL, *Classical,*
MARIA L. HARE,
EMMA M'LEAN,
EMMA M'CONNEL,
IRENE A. TAYLOR.

Class of 1865.

ANNIE M. GREGG, *Classical,*
REBECCA LAUCK,   "
SALLIE LINDSEY,
H. BELL. SCOTT,
JENNIE SCOTT,
RETTA D. SMITH.

Arcadia University's legacy began in 1853 when Sylvania (Jones) Stevens (1838–October 10, 1888) and Juliet A. (Poundstone) Avery (September 19, 1836–January 9, 1914), along with several other students, left their family homes in Fayette County, Pennsylvania, and accompanied Reverend Baker to the seminary. Graduating in 1856, they were the first students to receive diplomas from the Beaver Female Seminary. The Jones Poundstone Society, organized in 2019 in their honor, recognizes donors who support Arcadia's mission and enable the university to uphold its long-standing tradition of academic excellence, cutting-edge innovation, and groundbreaking initiatives. This image is from the *Eleventh Annual Catalogue of the Beaver Female Seminary and Musical Institute for the Session 1865–66.* (Arcadia University Archives.)

Beaver College and Musical Institute.

This Institution, now in the thirty-second year of its history, and in the twenty-seventh under the direction of the present incumbent of the Presidency, is pleasantly situated in the beautiful town of Beaver, the County Seat of Beaver County. It is twenty-six miles below Pittsburgh, on the bank of the Ohio, which consists here of a broad plateau, elevated one hundred feet above the bed of the river. This secures thorough drainage, and therefore renders the town proverbially healthful.

THE MOST EXTENSIVE BUILDINGS

Of any exclusively Ladies' School west of the mountains. The rooms are airy and cheerful, a perfect contrast to many contracted, gloomy rooms that are offered as homes for young ladies in too many schools, especially in the cities.

THE FACULTY

Consists of experienced Professors and Teachers, who are in the prime and vigor of life, and are fitted to give the most thorough training and careful attention to pupils in every department.

THE MUSIC DEPARTMENT,

Which has long been the most prominent of any of the schools in this section of the country, offers the very best advantages for the careful and critical pursuit of this important branch of a young lady's education. The Piano and Pipe Organ, Cabinet Organ, Violin, Banjo and Guitar, Voice Culture and Vocal Music receive attention from experienced and skillful teachers.

THE PIPE ORGAN

Is one of Hook & Hasting's best for its size, has two manuals, and was manufactured in Boston for the Institution.

ELOCUTION.

Classes who pay tuition in other departments receive instruction in this branch gratis, and Private Lessons are given at reasonable rates, naturalness and individuality being sought by the Professor.

THE ART DEPARTMENT

Embraces Drawing, Crayoning and Portraits, Water Colors, including fruit and flowers, Oil Colors and China Decorations, to which special attention is given. Pupils in this department are able to devote all their time to this if they choose to do so, thus making rapid progress. Send for Circular to the President,

REV. R. T. TAYLOR, Beaver, Pa.

Spring Term opens April 5, 1887. Fall Term, September 13, 1887.

In 1860, the name of the school was changed to Beaver Seminary and Institute. In 1865, the department of music was added to the curriculum, and the name of the school was updated to Beaver Seminary and Music Institute. (Beaver County Genealogy and History Center Collection.)

Around 1860, Pres. Riley Treadway Taylor (June 29, 1826–November 1, 1909) was instrumental in having the President's House built (pictured). The brick Italianate-style house, constructed across the street from the seminary, featured paired elongated windows, central gables with deep eaves supported by paired brackets, and a cupola. Since 1926, the house has been the home of the Fort McIntosh Club, and it still stands today. (Beaver County Genealogy and History Center Collection.)

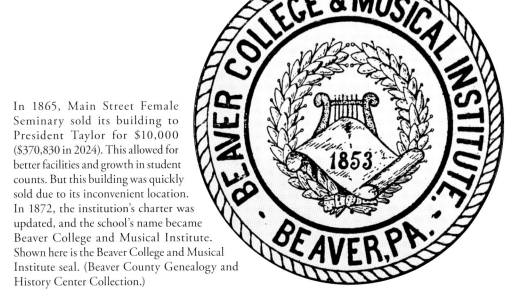

In 1865, Main Street Female Seminary sold its building to President Taylor for $10,000 ($370,830 in 2024). This allowed for better facilities and growth in student counts. But this building was quickly sold due to its inconvenient location. In 1872, the institution's charter was updated, and the school's name became Beaver College and Musical Institute. Shown here is the Beaver College and Musical Institute seal. (Beaver County Genealogy and History Center Collection.)

In 1872, the original building, constructed in 1855, was improved upon. An additional building nearly twice the size of the original was also built. Eventually, they were both connected. It included a chapel, practice rooms, and a hall with seating for 400. The ground on which these buildings stood was made up of two acres, and the remainder was given as recreational grounds for students. (Beaver County Genealogy and History Center Collection.)

In 1872, male students were admitted, and the college became coeducational for the first time. In 1907, when the school's name was shortened to Beaver College, enrollment was again limited to women; it would be nearly 60 years (1973) until men would again be welcome as part of the student body. This image is from *Caldwell's Illustrated, Historical, Centennial Atlas of Beaver County, 1876.* (Author's collection.)

The main building at Beaver College was destroyed on the morning of February 23, 1895, due to a devastating fire. Smoke can be seen rising from the burned-out structure in this image. Firefighters were helpless in fighting the blaze due to all water sources being frozen. (Arcadia University Archives.)

The fire, per newspaper records, was said to have started in the attic. Luckily, there were no casualties, and some of the building's contents were able to be saved. Students and on-site faculty were housed with area families, and classes were held in area churches and businesses. (Arcadia University Archives.)

Two structures replaced the one destroyed by the fire. The new College Hall, on the left, was dedicated in December 1895, and the Women's Residence Hall, on the right, was dedicated in 1897. After Beaver College's move to Jenkintown in 1925, the College Hall building continued on as Beaver High School (dedicated on November 11, 1927). After 1959, it was used as a junior high school and for administrative offices until it was razed in 1980. (Author's collection.)

In 1896, Pittsburgh Female College merged with Beaver College in Beaver, Pennsylvania, under the supervision of the Pittsburgh Conference of Methodist Episcopal Church. Pittsburgh Female College's assets were transferred to Beaver College, and many students and faculty continued to study at Beaver College. This image is from *Illustrated Atlas of the Upper Ohio River and Valley from Pittsburgh, Pa. to Cincinnati, Ohio: From United States Official and Special Surveys, 1877.* (Author's collection.)

The back of this photograph states, "18 graduates Class of 1897 Beaver College for Women, Beaver PA." The picture was taken from the steps of the Women's Residence Hall. Although the institution's charter was updated and the school's name became Beaver College and Musical Institute in 1872, it was not until 1903 that the University Senate of the Methodist Episcopal Church updated the school's classification from seminary to college. (Author's collection.)

VIEW ALONG COLLEGE AVENUE.

In April 1907, the stockholders of Beaver College and Musical Institute unanimously decided to amend the institution's charter to read "for the education of women" instead of "for the education of persons of both sexes" and to change the name from Beaver College and Musical Institute to Beaver College. The change went into effect at the close of the 1907 school year. (Beaver County Genealogy and History Center Collection.)

Higher Ground

SEVENTY years ago men saw a vision of an educational institution at Beaver. And so it was established. It has had some ups; and a pretty large share of downs.

Speaking with absolute frankness there have been people, who many times have thought it should be closed and the effort abandoned. But what right have we to abandon an institution that is needed when it is in our power to make it what it should be and what Western Pennsylvania wants?

For years Beaver College has struggled along, some-times seeming to prosper, oftentimes having a harder time than it deserved. Now those in authority say "Higher Ground." They and we all are determined—do or die—to reach that level for Beaver College.

The new campus on the hill west of Beaver is indeed high ground. Right now Beaver College must have the financial resources that will enable it in its courses of study, its buildings, faculty and its total environment to reach a level as high figuratively as the summit of its campus is in actuality.

And so it is higher ground for Beaver.

The *Beaver College Bulletin* from January 23, 1923, discusses the desire and plan to move and expand the grounds into a 100-acre campus of the new Beaver College. "The hundreds of young women who are turned

Back it up! Build it up!

THE Trustees of Beaver College voted authority for $1,250,000 for a new Beaver College. The Pittsburgh Annual Conference supplemented that with a vote equally progressive, quite as strong and forward looking.

Bishop Francis J. McConnell and District Superintendents are giving time, strength, cooperation, brains, leadership to this Movement.

Pastors and laymen are organized by Districts and Groups to practical working efficiency. The office in the Administration Hall has been busy for weeks doing the clerical work without which no organization can proceed. Publicity has begun and increases in extent and intensity.

All of these things are good for nothing—just a waste of money and time —unless you back it up.

Leadership, machinery, organization, publicity, can accomplish nothing and get nowhere, alone. They never

yet financed a college, though they have been governing factors in placing many millions in the treasuries of our colleges and universities.

It's up to us who believe in Beaver College to back it up and build it up! There is no use to talk students, or standardization, or courses of study, or faculties, or expansion, until we first talk money. $1,250,000 is as fundamental to students, faculty and class rooms of Beaver College as oxygen is fundamental to life.

With official authorization, with leaders in tune, the rest of us fairly enthusiastic over the new prospect, it is the auspicious time for every one of us to go deep into our check books, far into our pocketbooks to back up Beaver College and build it up to its best.

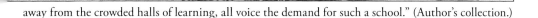

away from the crowded halls of learning, all voice the demand for such a school." (Author's collection.)

Seen here is the front side of a postcard that was used for the 1923 "Forward Look" fund-raising campaign. It shows a drawing of Beaver College's proposed new campus on Windy Ghoul, a hill overlooking Beaver, Pennsylvania. Today, this location is a large housing development. (Arcadia University Archives.)

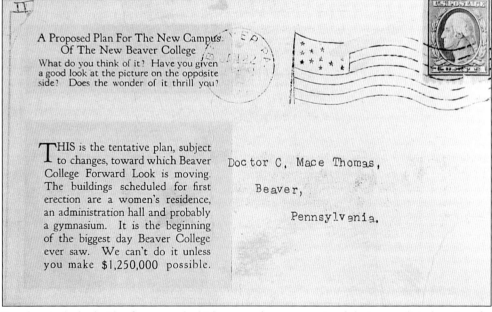

Seen here is the back side of a postcard which was used as a promotional device to solicit donations for the 1923 "Forward Look" fund-raising campaign. The plan failed when the $1.25 million ($22,345,833 in 2024) needed to complete it did not materialize, forcing the college to begin looking for another home and cut ties with the Methodist Episcopal Church. (Arcadia University Archives.)

Through its merger with Beechwood School in 1925, Beaver College found a new home with 11 acres in Jenkintown, Pennsylvania, purchased for $220,000 ($3,842,975 in 2024). In 1918, Beechwood School was advertised as "not just developing women of culture and personality but doing far more. They discover each student's ambitions and aptitudes along practical lines and fit her for employment which she may need or desire to pursue later in life. No daughter should be left unprepared." (Author's collection.)

Beechwood School opened in 1912 as a women's junior college and preparatory school. The Beechwood School location afforded larger facilities, an adequate campus, and greater development opportunities, which increased enrollment but maintained the advantages of a small college. The 1927 Beaver College yearbook mentions that Beechwood alumnae were welcomed and included in Beaver College alumni events going forward. This image is from the *Philadelphia Inquirer* on May 23, 1925. (Author's collection.)

EDUCATIONAL MERGER

Beechwood School at Jenkintown and Beaver College United

Announcement is made that Beechwood School, at Jenkintown, and Beaver College, Beaver, Pa., have been merged. With the end of the present term, the identity of Beechwood College will be submerged, and the institution continued under the title of Beaver College.

Coincident with the statement of the merger, the Old York Road Chamber of Commerce will sponsor a movement to aid the new college in the plan to raise a total of $250,000, to be applied to building purposes, conditional upon the obtaining of an endowment fund to aggregate $1,250,000 within the next three years.

Beechwood Inn, pictured here, became the main building of Beechwood School and was known as Beechwood Hall. After the merger of Beechwood School and Beaver College, the building was known as Reaser Hall. Before being purchased by Beechwood School, this building, constructed in the 1870s, was a summer hotel. Ledgers of architect Horace Trumbauer state that he was hired to make alterations to the inn in 1894. (Author's collection.)

A new dormitory was constructed for Beaver College after its relocation to the Jenkintown campus. The building, named Ryder Hall and later renamed Montgomery House, provided home-like surroundings for 64 students, as well as several members of the faculty. Features of the new building were suites for eight students, four bedrooms accommodating two students each, along with an accompanying sitting room. This image was published in the October 18, 1926, *Campus Crier*. (Arcadia University Archives.)

The *Bulletin of Beaver College* of April 1931 stated, "Spacious porches and an attractive landscape provide a pleasing atmosphere (South Porch–Reaser Hall)." Reaser Hall was named in honor of Dr. Mathew Howell Reaser, the founder and president of the former Beechwood School. Reaser Hall was renamed Beaver Hall in 1936. (Author's collection.)

According to the *Bulletin of Beaver College*, "The entrance to Reaser Hall is homelike and inviting (The Reception Hall)." The former use of the Beechwood name (for the inn, hall, and school) was due to the large amount of white beech trees that grew on the property. (Author's collection.)

Also written in the *Bulletin of Beaver College*, "The first floor of Reaser Hall contains music and fine art studios, offices, and a large, well-lighted dining room (Hallway to the Dining Room)." No undignified conduct or singing was allowed in the dining rooms. (Author's collection.)

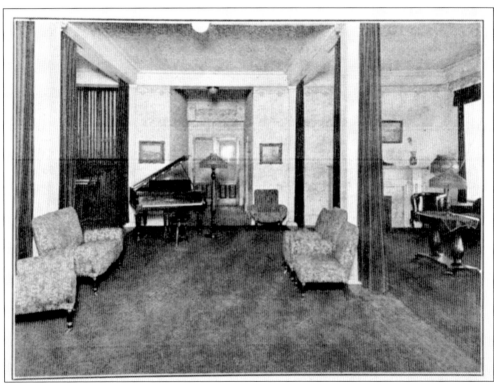

"Lounges are provided for the convenience of the students in entertaining callers, and for informal social gatherings of the students (One of the Lounges)," according to the *Bulletin of Beaver College*. Students were allowed to receive callers on Friday and Saturday evenings from 8:00 to 10:30 p.m. and Sunday for dinner and from 2:00 to 4:30 p.m. if they had filed written parent/guardian permission with the social directress. (Author's collection.)

Published in the *Bulletin of Beaver College*, "Sun Porch offers a warm cheerfulness on winter days (The Sun Porch)." Many of these porches at Reaser Hall would be enclosed and used as college administrative offices in the future. (Author's collection.)

Also in the *Bulletin of Beaver College*, "Good food, in bright surroundings, is a strong factor in health and happiness (A Dining Room–Jenkintown Campus)." The dining room was located on the main floor of Reaser Hall. Part of the dining hall was also used as the infirmary for a period of time. (Author's collection.)

"There are more than sixty private baths in connection with rooms or suites on the Jenkintown Campus. The dormitories are comfortable and are conveniently located (A suite with bath–Ryder Hall)," was also published in the *Bulletin of Beaver College*. (Author's collection.)

The *Bulletin of Beaver College* stated, "The chapel in Taylor Hall is equipped with a three-manual pipe organ and a Steinway piano. The sloping floor permits good vision from each seat (Chapel–Taylor Hall)." The hall was named after Pres. Riley T. Taylor, who served as president of the college from 1859 to 1894. (Author's collection.)

The article in *Bulletin of Beaver College* goes on: "In 1930 an addition was made to one of the buildings to provide larger facilities for the expanding library. The large reading room is well lighted and ventilated, has a potential seating capacity of two hundred and shelving space which can be expanded to accommodate 30,000 volumes (The College Library and Reading Room)." This was located in Huntington Hall. (Author's collection.)

"The Commercial Education–Secretaryship Department is fully equipped with typewriters, typewriter desks, files, bookkeeping and penmanship tables (A class in Commercial Education–Secretaryship)," was published in the *Bulletin of Beaver College* of April 1931. (Author's collection.)

Also according to the *Bulletin of Beaver College*, "The Health Education Department is provided with two gymnasiums, an indoor tennis court, outdoor tennis courts a swimming pool, basketball courts and athletic fields (A class in Health Education)." (Author's collection.)

BEAVER COLLEGE

For Women   *Founded* 1853
Continuing the Work of BEECHWOOD

At Jenkintown, Pa. Suburb of Philadelphia, two miles from city limits. A college of the cultural and practical. Diploma and degree courses in all departments. Courses extended, faculty enlarged, equipment increased. General College course, Junior College course, Music, Art, Kindergarten, Home Economics, Physical Education, Public School Music. States grant teaching certificates on special diplomas. Swimming pool, gymnasium, large new pipe organ. Catalog. Full degree rights. Address Registrar, Beechwood Hall, Beaver College.

Beechwood Hall

BEECHWOOD HILL SCHOOL
Sub-freshman Grade
(*Affiliated with Beaver College*)

New Dormitory — every bedroom with bath attached. Living Room and Sun Parlor for every eight resident students — a unique feature. All the advantages of a large institution with the personal care and individual attention of a small school. Strong faculty. College preparatory; training for home or good positions. Music; Art; Expression; Cooking; Sewing; Gymnasium; Swimming Pool; Athletic Grounds. Definitely fixed moderate rate. Address, Beechwood Hill School, Jenkintown, Pa.

Pictured is a c. 1926 Beaver College Jenkintown Campus advertisement. Other advertisements from this time state, "Every course based on student's individual aptitude or talent. Many graduates occupy positions of responsibility. General College course, Junior College course, Music, Art, Illustration, Design, Interior Decoration, Physical Education, Kindergarten-Primary, Expression, Public School Music, Home Economics, Secretaryship. States grant teaching certificates on special diplomas. Swimming pool, athletic field, gymnasium, library, large new pipe organ. Rates moderate." (Author's collection.)

BEAVER HALL, BEAVER COLLEGE, JENKINTOWN, PENNA.

Seen here is a postcard of Beaver Hall. Many rules governed how students were to act in the dormitories, such as, "There shall be absolute quiet in the buildings from 10.30 p.m. until 7.30 a.m.. There shall be no unnecessary noise in the residences or reception halls during quiet hours from 7.45–10.00 p.m. Sunday quiet all day. Quiet and dignified conduct is expected at all times. Quiet hour bell is rung at 7.45, after which time everyone is required to stay out of the halls." Students pledged to the following: "SELF-GOVERNMENT PLEDGE: I hereby pledge my honor as a student of Beaver College to abide by the regulations of Beaver College, and the Students Self-Government Association thereof, and that I will do no dishonest work in or out of classes, and that for protection to myself and loyalty to my fellow students of Beaver College I will report to the Executive Council of the Association any dishonest work or violation of any of said regulations that come to my notice." This pledge was listed in the 1929–1930 *Beaver College Handbook*. (Author's collection.)

To meet the need to house the growing student population, Montgomery Hall, built in 1926, was expanded in 1935–1937 in order to increase its capacity from 64 to 134 students. This image is from the 1937 Beaver College yearbook. (Arcadia University Archives.)

A postcard of Montgomery Hall is seen here. Student nurses from Abington Memorial Hospital occupied rooms in Beaver, Ivy, and Montgomery Halls while Abington's dormitory for new nurses was being completed in 1942. Construction of the building had been delayed by the many shortages of material caused by the war, and Beaver had available dorm rooms due to the same reason. (Author's collection.)

Huntington Hall housed students, the Beaver Library, and the Huntington Gymnasium. In addition to the gym being used for athletic activities, it was also used for parties, dances, and for the college's annual song contest. This image appeared in the 1944 Beaver College yearbook. (Arcadia University Archives)

Ivy Hall, pictured here, housed students and the pool. Ivy Hall was used several times as a dormitory during summer semester sessions. In the 1940s, the archery team practiced on the archery range that was located on the stretch of lawn alongside Ivy Hall. (Author's collection.)

BEAVER COLLEGE, JENKINTOWN, PA.
Ivy Hall

HOME ECONOMICS HOUSE, BEAVER COLLEGE, JENKINTOWN, PENNA.

Home Economics House/Highland Hall is pictured here. The 1936 Beaver College yearbook states, "The Home Economics Club is composed of students majoring in Home Economics. Organized in the spring of 1935, to develop an interest in the Home Economics department, and to foster high ideals of home life. Each girl, as a member of the club, is endeavoring to uphold the motto of the club, As our girlhood is now so shall our womanhood be." (Author's collection.)

The bell donated by the class of 1938 is seen atop a pedestal on the left side of the entrance to Taylor Hall (Chapel). This bell was later moved to the Glenside Campus when the campuses were consolidated in 1962. This photograph is from the 1944 Beaver College yearbook. (Arcadia University Archives.)

This is a photograph of Florence Lodge, the president's house. The May 17, 1946, edition of the *Beaver News* announced that President Kistler would again be residing in Florence Lodge as a full-time president. Due to World War II, lower student enrollment, and limited finances, President Kistler was in a part-time president role from 1943 to 1946. This image appeared in the 1939 Beaver College yearbook. (Arcadia University Archives.)

This postcard of Beaver Hall was postmarked in 1951. The back of the card states "Just hated to see you leave without souvenirs. . . . So behold! We have titled this photo 'Stark Realism.' 'X' marks my cell." Upon a closer look, an "X" is on the third story, seventh window from the left. (Author's collection.)

Pictured is the official Beaver College Jenkintown seal. The plan was to relocate the college to the Glenside campus soon after the purchase, but the stock market crash of 1929, the Great Depression that followed, and World War II delayed the move. In 1963, after the move to Glenside, all of the remaining Jenkintown campus structures were razed to make way for new development. In 1965, the Beaver Hill Condominiums, which included 400 dwellings units in three mid-rise buildings, were constructed on the former Jenkintown Campus property. (Arcadia University Archives.)

Two

1881–1928

The Harrison Grey Towers Estate Prior to Beaver College's Glenside Campus

In 1881, William Welsh Harrison Sr. purchased Rosedale Hall from J. Thomas Audenreid. This estate was on the Willow Grove Turnpike/Limekiln Pike between Church Road and Rosedale Avenue in Cheltenham Township, Montgomery County, Pennsylvania. In 1892, modifications designed by Horace Trumbauer were made to Rosedale Hall. The home, originally constructed of wood, was encased in a stone facade, preserving the rooms of Rosedale Hall. Rosedale Hall and its contents were destroyed by a fire discovered at one o'clock in the morning of January 14, 1893. Harrison and his family had just enough time to escape from their beds. The thermometer stood at two degrees above zero, and the ground was covered with snow. They found shelter in the stables. Quickly, Trumbauer designed a new home for Harrison made of Chestnut Hill grey stone, with Indiana limestone trimmings. On the east and north, the building is surrounded by terraces paved with marble mosaic bordered by stone balustrades. On the south front, an open court enclosed with balustrades terminates into a stone stairway winding down to the carriage drive 10 feet below. When finished, the name of Grey Towers was found to be more appropriate than Rosedale Hall. After buying additional neighboring properties, Harrison eventually accumulated 138 acres. An interesting part of the university's folklore, and one that only adds to the many ghost stories that have been passed down from class to class, revolves around one of the parcels purchased by Harrison that included a church and a small cemetery. This parcel was on the lower part of the campus where the Classroom Building/Taylor Hall is located. A parsonage was built in 1875 for the Harmer Methodist Episcopal Church, and services were held there until 1899. Harrison purchased this land as part of his expansion plan for his estate, but litigation in court over the removal of the bodies from the cemetery complicated the sale. On November 1, 1905, court permission was obtained to remove the bodies and reinter them elsewhere. He removed the approximately 250 bodies, some of which had been there for a century, and had most of them reinterred at Hillside Cemetery in Abington.

William Welsh Harrison Sr. (May 5, 1850–March 4, 1927) co-owned the Franklin Sugar Refinery with his siblings. He purchased the 38-acre Rosedale Hall estate in Glenside, Pennsylvania, from John Thomas Audenreid (May 2, 1837–March 10, 1884) in 1881. He was married to Bertha Marie (Whyte) Harrison (1857–1933) in 1886. (Arcadia University Archives.)

The Franklin Sugar Refinery began construction in 1866 on Almond and Swanson Streets by the Delaware River in Philadelphia, Pennsylvania. Charles Custis Harrison (May 3, 1844–February 12, 1929), William's brother, founded the company. In 1892, the Harrisons sold their stock to H.O. Havemeyer and the American Sugar Refinery and left the business. The complex of buildings was removed to construct Interstate 95. This image came from Ernest Hexamer, Hexamer General Surveys, Vol. 30, Plates 2952–2953. (Author's collection.)

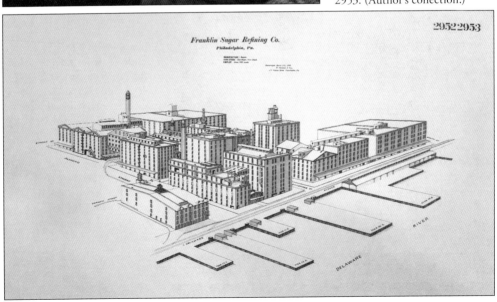

The Harrisons raised their children, Geraldine Dorothy (Harrison) Anderson (1880–1903) and William Welsh Harrison Jr. (1881–1965), pictured here, on the Glenside property. Geraldine married John Childe Anderson on March 14, 1902. She passed away on February 26, 1903, in Philadelphia (not at the castle as some university folklore states). Her body did lay in state at Grey Towers prior to being buried at Laurel Hill Cemetery in Philadelphia, Pennsylvania. (Arcadia University Archives.)

William Welsh Harrison Jr. (pictured here) was a member of the board of trustees for Abington Memorial Hospital and gave great financial support. The discrepancy between Geraldine's and William Jr.'s birthdates and William and Bertha's marriage date does not seem to have been explained, except that they were born before William and Bertha's marriage took place. There are no known images of Bertha Harrison. This image came from the 1904 University of Pennsylvania yearbook. (Arcadia University Archives.)

By 1891, William Harrison Sr. hired architect Horace Trumbauer (December 28, 1868–September 18, 1938), pictured here, to build a new stable, gatehouse, and powerhouse while modernizing the existing Rosedale Hall, costing $30,000 ($1,029,665 in 2024). This work was completed in 1892. Horace Trumbauer went on to become a prominent American architect of the Gilded Age, best known for designing residential manors for the wealthy in the Philadelphia area. (Arcadia University Archives.)

This postcard, postmarked 1908, shows the entrance and gatehouse to Grey Towers that was completed in 1892, prior to the castle's construction, costing $8,000 ($274,577 in 2024). This entrance included turrets and metal dragon guards to protect against unwelcome guests. (Author's collection.)

THE LODGE, ENTRANCE TO GRAY TOWERS. RESIDENCE OF W. W. HARRISON, GLENSIDE, PA.

ENTRANCE TO GREY TOWERS. GLENSIDE, PA.

Copyrighted and Pub. by G. Gold Parker, Wyncote, Pa.

This postcard, postmarked 1909, shows the entrance and gatehouse to Grey Towers that was completed in 1892, prior to the castle's construction. The gatehouse and stables are built in the medieval Norman style, with the stables receiving additional medieval French brickwork. (Author's collection.)

This is a view of the property around the carriage house/stables and clock tower with chimes (later Murphy Hall), completed in 1892, prior to the castle's construction, costing $100,000 ($3,432,219 in 2024). Rosedale Avenue is in the foreground on the left. (Later, the 309 Expressway would be located here.) In 1894, Horace Trumbauer drafted plans for the building of the clock tower on the stables, per the Trumbauer Ledger A, page 32. (Arcadia University Archives.)

This is another view of Murphy Hall. Note the dormers on the left side of the building's roof and the third-story windows pictured here, neither of which are present on the modern structure. This is due to a fire caused by a lightning strike that took place on the morning of May 1, 1920. The loss was estimated to be $100,000 ($1,538,945 in 2024). When rebuilt, the roof was simplified, and the window configuration was changed. (Arcadia University Archives.)

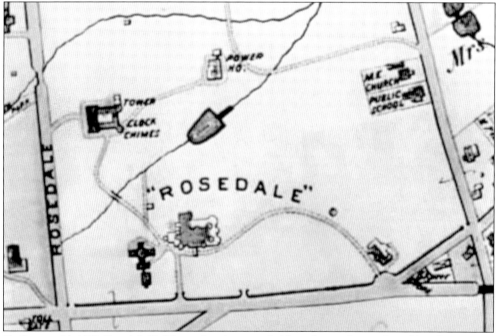

On January 14, 1893, Rosedale Hall burned to the ground. After taking refuge in the stables, the Harrison family moved into the gatehouse. Harrison again hired Trumbauer to build a new home on the site. By March 1893, Trumbauer presented Harrison with plans for a lavish mansion. Work was underway by the end of 1893. The construction took five years. This image came from *North Penn Atlas*, published by A.H. Mueller in 1897. (Author's collection.)

The grey stone used to construct the castle was quarried in nearby Chestnut Hill, near Germantown Avenue and Cresheim Road. Indiana limestone was crafted into exterior trim for doors, windows, and other elements. Craftsmen, local and far away, were called upon due to the vast amount of stone and woodwork involved in the details of Grey Towers, completed in the fall of 1898. Harrison owned what would eventually be known as one of America's great castles. (Author's collection.)

This postcard, postmarked 1908, shows Grey Towers and the Solarium/Conservatory. Inspired by Alnwick Castle, the medieval seat of the Dukes of Northumberland, the new house would include all the most modern conveniences of the time. The cost was estimated at $250,000 ($8,491,416 in 2024). With its 41 rooms, it also was one of the largest homes in the country. (Author's collection.)

This postcard, postmarked 1909, shows Grey Towers and the Solarium/Conservatory. The floor plan is that of an "L," measuring roughly 166 by 174 feet exclusive of terraces, with the main entrance on the east front within the Porte Cochere. (Author's collection.)

Open terraces line part of the east and west walls. Joining at their northern ends is a covered terrace along the north front. Another, deeper terrace with balustrades runs along a portion of the south front with a double-curving stairway of limestone descending to the drive. (Author's collection.)

This postcard, postmarked 1910, shows the south lawn of Grey Towers and the group of smaller buildings constructed of iron framework and glass. The Willow Grove & Germantown Turnpike/Limekiln Pike is seen running along the front of the property. (Author's collection.)

All roofs on the castle are flat, concealed by crenellations. From the towers rise smaller towers also topped with crenellations. Student access to the roof is not allowed, but in the past, there was limited access, as many students used the rooftop as a setting for their yearbook senior portraits. This image is from the 1980 Beaver College yearbook. (Arcadia University Archives.)

The castle features several functional hand-carved ornate gargoyles, as well as many interesting grotesques and other architectural carvings. The picture here is one of the many gargoyles hand carved in Indiana limestone. Because they are hand carved, no two are alike. (Author's collection.)

In architecture, and specifically Gothic architecture, a gargoyle is a carved or formed grotesque with a spout designed to convey water from a roof and away from the side of a building, thereby preventing it from running down masonry walls and eroding the mortar between. Pictured here are a pair of gargoyles that are present on the castle. (Author's collection.)

In architecture, the term "grotesque" refers to a decorative carved stone figure. Grotesques are often confused with gargoyles, but the distinction is that gargoyles are figures that contain a waterspout, typically through the mouth, while grotesques do not. Seen here is a grotesque. (Author's collection.)

Many scholars describe grotesques as being used to ward off evil and as reminders of the separation of the earth from the divine. This type of sculpture is also known as a chimera when it depicts fantastical creatures. Pictured are a pair of grotesques that are present on the castle. (Author's collection.)

Two of these intimidating griffin figures sat guard on the Gatehouse Arch. At one time, a heavy chain was strung between them to keep individuals from entering the property. Yearbook photographs after 1968 no longer show them present on the arch. (Arcadia University Archives.)

Many of these copper griffin figures sat along the rim of the castle's Solarium/Conservatory, which was removed in 1952. A few still stand guard on the glass vestibule that remains. In addition, the university archives hold a few of the griffin figures in their collection. (Arcadia University Archives.).

Just within the east entrance to the castle, the interior is dominated by a main hall rising three stories to a coffered, barrel-vaulted ceiling in the style of the French Renaissance. Galleries surround the hall on three sides on the second- and third-floor levels. At the west end, a grand mahogany stairway rises to a landing (the Music Room) and divides right and left to the second-floor gallery. This image is from the 1940 Beaver College yearbook. (Arcadia University Archives.)

The Music Room opens through a large archway onto the landing. All woodwork in the main hall and music room is mahogany, hand carved in French Renaissance style. Large leaded Belgian windows add to the ambiance of the space. The mantel in the Music Room is clearly inspired by one of the mantels from the Salle des Gardes in the Château de Blois. This photograph appeared in the 1951 Beaver College yearbook. (Arcadia University Archives.)

On the first-floor level in the north and south walls of the main hall, there are two large fireplaces framed in marble with mantels of limestone, closely mimicking the lines of the other mantel from the Salle des Gardes in the Château de Blois. The barrel-vaulted ceiling is studded with electric lights and has eight skylights in the center. This image is from the 1940 Beaver College yearbook. (Arcadia University Archives.)

American-made tapestries produced by the firm of Baumgarten (signed and dated 1898) are set above the wainscoting in the Music Room. *The Bronx River in History & Folklore* states, "A larger order still, fourteen pieces in all, went to Grey Towers, the new home of industrialist William Welsh Harrison in Glenside, Pennsylvania. The set remains intact to this day." This image appeared in the 1974 Beaver College yearbook. (Arcadia University Archives.)

William Harrison Sr.'s sitting area and library were located to the left of the castle's main entrance. Since 1962, this area has been used as the phone operator's station and the President's Office suite. Pictured is the President's Office, with Pres. Edward D. Gates sitting behind the desk. The ceiling is coffered, and below the ceiling cornice, there is a molded plaster frieze with cupids and garlands. (Arcadia University Archives.)

Pictured here is the West/Ball/Mirror Room. The entire room was ordered as a package through a French firm in 1900 at a cost of $19,000 ($709,215 in 2024). The ceiling depicts the four seasons as women, attended by cupids, floating against a sky cut by the path of the zodiac. Within the cove separating the walls from the ceiling runs a vine motif ornamented with cupids, long-necked birds, and female figures. (Arcadia University Archives.)

Pictured here is the East/Drawing/Rose Room, showing the Harrisons' possessions prior to Beaver College's purchase in 1929. It is called the Rose Room due to ceiling paintings that include cupids holding roses. (Courtesy of the National Register of Historic Places.)

This view of the East/Drawing/Rose Room shows the Harrisons' possessions prior to Beaver College's purchase in 1929. It adjoins the Mirror Room through a pair of sliding doors. The room is ungilded, and the ornamentation is considered typical of the late Louis XV style. In one corner, there is a fireplace with a carved marble mantel. The paintings and wall fabrics in this room were all produced by the Baumgarten Company. (Arcadia University Archives.)

This is a 1929 view of Bertha Harrison's bedroom (second floor, southeast corner) with the Harrisons' possessions still in place. There is documentation in the university's archives that states there was a large bird cage that housed 1,000 canaries in the front window on the second floor of the castle. (Courtesy of the National Register of Historic Places.)

This 1929 view of the main hall looks north, with the Harrisons' possessions still in place. Hidden behind the grand stairway on a sunken landing, a half-level below the Great Hall, was William Harrison's Billiard Room. In the 1930s, the college converted this to an apartment for the castle housemother and, later, the director of residence. This room was furnished and configured in such a way that it served as a bedroom for the housemother/residence director, provided a living room where she could entertain students and guests, and even contained a small kitchenette for preparing meals. (Courtesy of the National Register of Historic Places.)

This is a 1930s view of the main hall looking north toward the Mirror and Rose Rooms. On the landing of the stairway, a large archway provides entrance into the Music Room. Each pier of the arch has a mahogany mask, drapery swags, musical instruments, and a cupid. The mahogany mantel, like those in the great hall, was derived from the Salle des Gardes at the Château de Blois. (Author's collection.)

Seen here is a 1929 view of the Dining Room with the Harrisons' possessions still in place. The college used this space for student and faculty meals until the Dining Hall space attached to Dilworth Hall was constructed in 1962. The Breakfast Room is located west of the Dining Room, attached by a corridor. The walls have walnut paneling with tapestries of hunt scenes above. (Arcadia University Archives.)

This 1929 view of the South Front Lawn shows the Solarium/Conservatory, designed by Horace Trumbauer. In 1900, Harrison hired Trumbauer to design a ballroom, and in 1907, the circular, glass Solarium/Conservatory on the south terrace with an adjoining aviary was built. (Arcadia University Archives.)

Seen here is a 1929 view of the South Front Lawn showing details of the Greenhouses/Laboratories. Originally, the college had plans to use these structures as part of the campus's daily activities, but they were removed in the early 1930s. (Arcadia University Archives.)

This is a 1929 view of the Rose Arbor. This arbor was originally part of the Harrison Estate. The Rose Arbor was a meeting place for the senior-class Lantern Chain Ceremony, as mentioned in the June 6, 1941, and June 5, 1942, *Beaver News*. The arbor was located near the main entrance of the Landman Library, northwest of where the wishing well is located today. (Arcadia University Archives.)

This view looks up toward the back of the castle from where the pond was located (near where Brubaker Hall is located today). Sheep were commonly used to keep lawns manicured. There were great advantages to the usage of sheep, as they also aerated the lawn with their hooves and spread fertilizer in the form of urine and manure. (Arcadia University Archives.)

This early-1900s view looking southeast shows the original entrance of the Harrison Estate (south corner). The stable/carriage house can be seen in the background. To the left of the column is Rosedale Avenue, where the 309 Expressway would eventually be constructed. This entrance is no longer in existence. (Arcadia University Archives.)

Pictured from the same location as before but looking north toward the south lawn are Grey Towers and the group of smaller buildings constructed of iron framework and glass. This entrance is no longer in existence. (Arcadia University Archives.)

Pictured is an original entrance to Harrison's estate in front of the castle. Grey Towers and the Solarium/Conservatory can be seen in the background. Today, this is the location for the main entrance to the campus on Easton Road/Limekiln Pike. (Arcadia University Archives.)

Farther to the right was an additional original entrance located in front of where Kistler Hall is today. This picture is from the 1980s. It is a later view of the entrance that is shown on the cover of this book. This entrance is no longer in existence. (Arcadia University Archives.)

Seen here is a 1950s view showing an original entrance (including the gatehouse and the arch) that would have been considered the main point of entry when visiting the Harrison family. Today, this entrance is only available for foot and bike traffic. (Arcadia University Archives.)

This 1950s view shows the east corner and another entrance to the Harrison Estate looking north. This part of the campus was all open space, as no buildings or parking lots were constructed in this area until 1962. The road on the right side of the picture is Church Road. This entrance is no longer in existence. (Arcadia University Archives.)

This complex of buildings (the Benton Spruance Art Center) is part of the original Harrison Estate and was constructed prior to Grey Towers. It consisted of a powerhouse with a smokestack (currently the Spruance Art Gallery), a carpenter shop (currently the Little Theater), a machine shop and office (currently a wood shop), and a battery storage building (currently classrooms for the fine arts department). (Arcadia University Archives.)

The powerhouse structure had two underground pipes/tunnels that disseminated from it, which provided water, electricity, and steam to the castle and Murphy Hall. There is still a fully intact pipe/tunnel leading from Murphy Hall to the powerhouse. The powerhouse was built with redundancies, as there were two of every component, two dynamos, and two furnaces. If one failed, the other would be put into use. (Arcadia University Archives.)

Pictured here in 2023 is the second partial pipe/tunnel, which still runs from the castle to the Commons (this tunnel was intercepted and terminated because of the Commons construction in 2010). Prior to the Commons construction, this tunnel went to the former powerhouse structure (now the Spruance Art Center building). In the basement of the castle, a set of huge fans circulated cool air throughout the structure in the summer. Note the large steel door that acts as the entrance to the tunnel from the basement in the castle. (Courtesy of Anastasia Rousseau, Arcadia University.)

WILLIAM W. HARRISON DIES.

Retired Sugar Refiner Was Socially Prominent in Philadelphia.

Special to The New York Times.

PHILADELPHIA, March 4.—William Welsh Harrison, retired sugar refiner and member of a socially prominent Philadelphia family, died yesterday at his home, Grey Towers, near Glenside, a suburb, following an attack of heart disease. He was 70 years old.

Mr. Harrison was a brother of Charles Custis Harrison, former Provost of the University of Pennsylvania. He recently appeared as plaintiff against his broker, Francis Ralston Welsh, in which Mr. Harrison charged that he was defrauded of $239,000 over a ten-year period.

Mr. Harrison, his brother Charles and William C. Frazier became copartners in the Franklin Sugar Refinery, but the former retired from business in 1892. He was a member of the Philadelphia Club and the University and Rittenhouse clubs. His wife, a son, William Harrison Jr., and three brothers survive him.

William Welsh Harrison Sr. died on March 4, 1927. The *Philadelphia Inquirer* of March 5, 1927, announced his passing at Grey Towers from heart issues. Other publications noted he had passed following a prolonged attack of the heart and that the fatal attack was induced by cold and acute indigestion. Note that the newspaper incorrectly states Harrison was 70 years of age at his death. He was actually 76, as correctly stated on the death certificate below. (Author's collection.)

A copy of his death certificate is seen at right. He is buried at the Laurel Hill Cemetery in Philadelphia, Pennsylvania, in a family crypt he shares with his wife, daughter, and son. Laurel Hill Cemetery is located in the East Falls neighborhood of Philadelphia. It was founded in 1836 and was the preferred burial ground of Philadelphia's rich and famous. (Arcadia University Archives.)

Three

1928–2001

Transformation of Beaver College

as an Institution

After William Welsh Harrison Sr. died in 1927, his wealth was distributed per his last will and testament. Harrison left large sums of money to institutions he cared about throughout his life. In addition, there was a publicized stipulation in his will, as printed in the March 14, 1927, *New York Times*: "Philadelphia, Pa., March 13. William Welsh Harrison Jr., at his home, Grey Towers, refused tonight to divulge the attitude that he and his mother would take toward the will of his father, a retired sugar refinery which makes outright bequests of more than $500,000 [$8,822,600 in 2024] and a provisionary gift of a similar amount to Mrs. Isabella S. Fishblatt, a wealthy widow of Atlantic City. The latter $500,000 gift is conditional upon the attitude the son takes toward marriage. In the event that he does not marry and leave heirs, this amount will go to Mrs. Fishblatt at his death and the rest of his share of the estate, valued at $4,000,000 [$70,580,690 in 2024] will benefit a group of educational and charitable institutions. Questioned as to whether the relatives would accept the will or court action would be taken, Mr. Harrison replied, 'I'm sorry, I can give you no information.' He would not indicate whether the provisions of the will would influence his attitude toward matrimony. Disclosures made since the filing of yesterday, the will at Norristown, however, show that the testator had made gifts to Mrs. Fishblatt before his death. It was recalled today that in a deposition read during Mr. Harrison's illness at a trial before Federal Judge Moskovitz in Brooklyn last June, the sugar refiner admitted having given to Mrs. Fishblatt 4,900 shares of preferred stock of the American Sugar Refining Company. Mrs. Fishblatt was suing a brokerage firm for the alleged loss of $600,000 [$10,587,100 in 2024] to her through an unauthorized sale of securities. At Mrs. Fishblatt's Atlantic City home servants said today that she was 'out of town' and that because of a death in the family she had not been receiving anybody for several days. Questioned about the death, they said it was a 'Mr. Harrison.' Doubt was expressed in some quarters here as to any attempt to break the Harrison will." Note that William Harrison Jr. never married, and his deceased sister's husband was not left anything in the will. In 1928–1929, Beaver College (now Arcadia University), then located in Jenkintown, purchased 23 acres of the estate from his widow for $712,500 ($12,737,125 in 2024). Classes were split between the two locations until 1962, when the college moved permanently to the Grey Towers property.

CAMPUS CRIER

Published Bi-Weekly by the Students of Beaver College

Vol. 4   THURSDAY, DECEMBER 6, 1928   No. 4

Beaver Buys the Well Known "Castle"

Much Talked of Deal Finally Put Through

Beaver College for Women at Jenkintown has purchased Grey Towers, the Glenside property of the W. W. Harrison estate, it was announced yesterday. The purchase is part of an expansion program developed since the induction of the Rev. Dr. Walter B. Greenway as president.

It is expected that the buildings on the estate will be adapted to their new use by next fall, although the final settlement of the property has been deferred. The amount of the purchase was not made known, although it is said that the buildings alne are insured for $1,765,000.

Grey Towers and its environs are modeled after Alnwick Castle, England. The lofty battlement can be seen for miles around and the castle is one of the showplaces of the East.

The towers was built in 1893 by William Welsh Harrison after fire had restroyed Rosedale, on the country estate of J. Thomas Audenried. Mr. Harrison's hobby was to plan further additions to the imposing buildings and to superintend personally the carrying out of his plans.

Six great towers, surmounted by massive battlements, divide the principal front. A costly stone gateway and picturesque gatehouse form the entrance from Church road. Even the stables are splendid in their design and the water and power plants are sufficient for a small town, it is said.

The interior decoration includes rare woods, tapestries and other art objects of great value. The ballroom, which will be converted into a chapel, will seat 1200 students, it is estimated. Fire in 1920 caused damage estimated at $75,000 to the servants' quarters, garage and carriage house.

The new addition will not replace, but will supplement, the present buildings at Jenkintown, Dr. Greenway said yesteerday. Grey Towers will provide dorimtory faciloities for at least 100 girls. The present student body of 500 will be raised to 750 in a few years' time.

Reprinted from the Philadelphia Public Ledger.

The Beaver College newspaper, the *Campus Crier*, dated December 6, 1928, announced the purchase of the Glenside property to the Beaver population (although the actual legal transaction did not take place until April 1929). (Arcadia University Archives.)

This *Campus Crier*, dated December 19, 1928, presents photographs of the Glenside property and Grey Towers to the student population. There was much excitement on the Jenkintown campus at this time of the fact that there was a castle on the property. (Arcadia University Archives.)

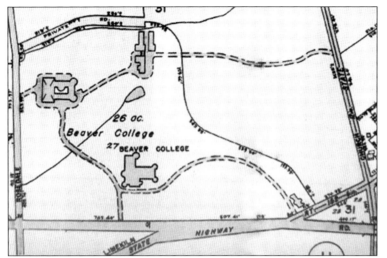

This map shows the initial 23 acres purchased by Beaver College. The college added to this property throughout the years. This image is from *Property Atlas of Montgomery County, Pennsylvania.* (Author's collection.)

Beaver College mailed the *Bulletin of Beaver College* of July 1929 to alumni and investors letting them know of the news. In the fall of 1929, sixty-five students were housed in the castle and fourteen in the gatehouse. The science department occupied space in the former stables. The remodeled hayloft became a chapel seating seven hundred with a gymnasium below. (Author's collection.)

This *Bulletin of Beaver College* also included a "Panoramic view of the Grey Towers Campus." Beaver College only purchased 26 acres from the Harrison Estate in 1928–1929. An additional 30 acres to the north of Grey Towers, following the lane leading from the gatehouse (the Alumni Fund Walk of Pride), was purchased in 1947. Beaver College was permitted to use the land by keeping it in good condition until the purchase was made. (Author's collection.)

Also in this issue of *Bulletin of Beaver College* was the "Main entrance to Campus." Today, this entrance is still in existence, but it is only open to bike and foot traffic. As of 2024, the arch is not in place due to structural and safety issues. (Author's collection.)

Seen here is the "Rear view of main building" in the July 1929 *Bulletin of Beaver College*. Grey Towers was officially dedicated by Beaver College on June 1, 1929, at 2:00 p.m. during the 75th Annual Commencement Program of Events. (Author's collection.)

Here is "The Porte Cochere" from the *Bulletin of Beaver College*. This is the view that guests would have had when approaching the castle entrance. Note the greenhouses viewed in the background through the Porte Cochere. (Author's collection.)

Pictured in the *Bulletin of Beaver College* is "The main entrance," which was on the east facade within the Porte Cochere. The doorway consists of wood-glazed double doors framed within an elaborate stone surround with Gothic detailing. Once inside the castle, one would be met by the sight of the awe-inspiring Great Hall. (Author's collection.)

Also in the *Bulletin of Beaver College* was this image of the "Artistic Bridge and main building." The property has many areas that are considered optimal for picture-taking. This view, which includes the Murphy Bridge (or "the Bridge to Murphy") and the castle, is a favorite to this day. (Author's collection.)

Another image published within the *Bulletin of Beaver College* was "Side view of Recitation Hall showing entrance to gymnasium." The building was later dedicated and named Murphy Memorial Hall. The first floor housed the gymnasium (originally the carriage house) and science laboratories. (Author's collection.)

Seen here is "Rear view of Recitation Hall showing Chimes Tower" from the July 1929 issue of *Bulletin of Beaver College*. The second floor housed the chapel and additional science laboratories. Murphy Chapel had three stained-glass windows installed in the early 1940s. They were designed by John W. Hathaway (1905–1987), who taught at Beaver College from 1934 until 1971. He is also recognized for his work as a painter and printmaker. (Author's collection.)

Also in the *Bulletin of Beaver College* was "The Laboratory" (or Greenhouse). The Laboratories were a group of smaller buildings constructed of iron framework and glass. Per the Grey Towers dedication program, these structures were to serve the needs of the chemistry, home economics, and domestic science departments. Plans changed when all of the structures were removed from the property within two years of the purchase. (Author's collection.)

Pictured in the *Bulletin of Beaver College* was the "Social Hall" (or Mirror Room). It is not known why Harrison desired such an impressive structure with large social spaces. It seems almost certain that the Harrisons intended to entertain their peers on a grand scale, but there is no evidence that such a social life ever developed. (Author's collection.)

From the *Bulletin of Beaver College* is this image, "A Bed Room." The second floor contained separate bedroom suites with dressing rooms, fireplaces, and marble baths for the Harrisons. The third floor contained several bedroom suites for the Harrisons' children, Geraldine and William Jr. (Author's collection.)

Published in the July 1929 *Bulletin of Beaver College* was this image of the "Faculty House and Art Studio" (today known as the Alumni House at Blankley Hall). This photograph was taken from inside the campus. The arch and the former main entrance to campus are shown here to the right. (Author's collection.)

MURPHY HALL

In 1929, Murphy Memorial Hall was presented by Jane M. Murphy in memory of her husband, William M. Murphy. At the time, an organ was also donated and installed in the chapel (later Stiteler Auditorium). The chorus made use of this area to practice and compete. Over the years, metalworking, photography, and ceramics studios were added. The organ was removed in the 1980s. (Author's collection.)

THE GYMNASIUM, MURPHY HALL

Murphy Memorial Hall once housed the stables where the Harrison family kept their horses and carriages. After the initial purchase of the land by Beaver College, the building was used for science labs. The building also included a gymnasium (pictured) with a shooting range for the school's rifle team. (Author's collection.)

In 1929, Beaver College was the proud recipient of a new organ in Murphy Chapel, donated by Jane M. Murphy. This instrument was an electric pneumatic three-manual organ. It was built by F.A. Bartholomay & Sons Organ Builders of Philadelphia, Pennsylvania. The entire cost was $9,000 ($160,890 in 2024). The college felt fortunate to have received this gift and extended sincere appreciation. This image is from the 1930 Beaver College yearbook. (Arcadia University Archives.)

The Murphy Memorial Chapel became the Stiteler Memorial Presbyterian Chapel in 1976–1977 (named after benefactor Frederick D. Stiteler). Later, the space would be known as the Stiteler Auditorium. The auditorium had stadium seating with classic red velvet theater chairs. Stained-glass windows lined the walls. In most recent decades, Stiteler Auditorium was used for the theater program, hosting many events. All remaining remnants of the chapel/auditorium were removed in 2022. (Author's collection.)

DUCK POND — GREY TOWERS.
BEAVER COLLEGE. JENKINTOWN. PENNA.

A brook and pond, known as Alnwick Brook and Alnwick Pool (named after Alnwick Castle in the English county of Northumberland, from which Grey Towers received its inspiration), once existed at the bottom of the hill behind Grey Towers where Brubaker Hall stands today. The brook and pond dried up when the stream feeding them was dammed by the construction of the Pennsylvania Route 309 bypass in the spring of 1959. (Author's collection.)

At one time, there was a Solarium/ Conservatory constructed of glass and metal on the patio located on the south side of Grey Towers. It was designed by architect Horace Trumbauer and constructed in 1907. This image is from the 1937 Beaver College yearbook. (Arcadia University Archives.)

This photograph shows the inside view of the Solarium/Conservatory. Unfortunately, the Conservatory was removed in 1952 due to its unsafe and deteriorating condition. No parts of the Conservatory are known to survive except for a few of the copper figures that sat along the outside of the rim of the roof. These are part of the university archives collection. This image is from the 1940 Beaver College yearbook. (Arcadia University Archives.)

This photograph shows the same view of the patio as above but after the Solarium/Conservatory was removed in 1952. Later, this sunken bird bath/fountain would be removed too. Today this area is an open patio. This image originally appeared in the 1954 Beaver College yearbook. (Arcadia University Archives.)

The well, built as part of the Harrison Estate, originally had a thatched roof as pictured. It still stands today, located near the Dining Hall Complex. Currently, it has a shingle roof and houses a bell (a gift from the class of 1938). This bell once hung outside of Taylor Hall Chapel on the Jenkintown campus. The bell itself, known as the "Virginity Bell," has a scandalous tradition behind it. This picture is from the 1931 Beaver College yearbook. (Arcadia University Archives.)

This is a picture of a second well located on the campus property. It is believed that this well was dug for a separate property Harrison accumulated while expanding his acreage. Once under his ownership, he had Horace Trumbauer design the grand structure seen here. Per the Trumbauer Ledger B, page 133, it was constructed of Indiana limestone. No part of this well is believed to still be present on the campus property. The 1916 A.H. Mueller *Atlas of North Penn Pennsylvania*, Plate 7, labels the well as "Old Oaken Bucket." This image is from the 1950 Beaver College yearbook. (Arcadia University Archives)

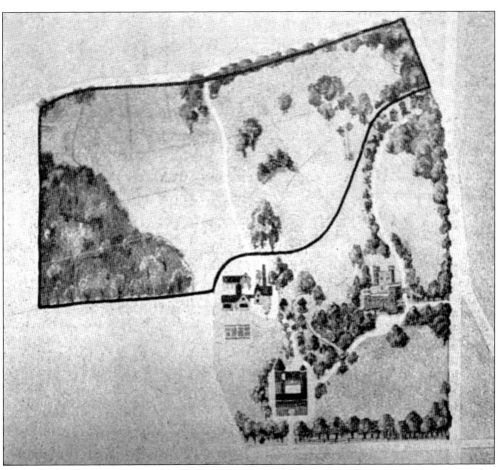

Shown here is a map as presented in the February 28, 1947, issue of the *Beaver News* announcing that the college had purchased an additional 30 acres for the Glenside campus. The article states that the college now had a total of 56 acres to move forward with the campus consolidation plan. (Arcadia University Archives.)

The September 30, 1955, *Beaver News* reported, "Dr. Morgan Thomas lays Cornerstone of Centennial Hall on Grey Towers Campus. With the corner-laying ceremonies on the Grey Towers campus, a dream of the consolidated campus in Glenside came closer to reality." The architects for this building were Martin, Stewart, and Noble. Dr. Thomas and Vira Heinz, trustees and benefactors, assumed the payment of the Grey Towers property's mortgage during World War II. (Arcadia University Archives.)

The article goes on: "The new dormitory, to be called Centennial Hall, is partly completed and is expected to be finished early in the spring of 1956. The building's name is thought to be appropriate as it is the first new structure built for the campus in its second century." (Arcadia University Archives.)

After Dr. Morgan H. Thomas's passing in the summer of 1956, Centennial Hall's name was changed to Thomas Hall, and the dormitory was dedicated in his honor. This dorm allowed for the housing of an additional 62 students on the Glenside campus. The cost was $260,000 ($2,978,610 in 2024) plus an additional $30,000 ($343,690 in 2024) for furnishings. Pictured is the interior of a Thomas Hall dorm room. (Arcadia University Archives.)

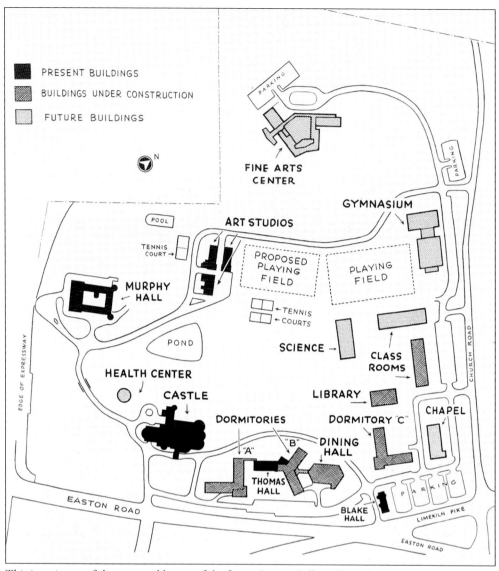

This is an image of the proposed layout of the future Beaver College Glenside Campus, as presented in the *Gateway to Tomorrow* brochure created by the college in 1962. This brochure mentions that "Beaver College emphasizes the relevance of a liberal education to the increasing variety of services women perform in our society, including the guiding and shaping of the future generation, whose intellectual and cultural values largely will be determined in the home." Karl T. Weger headed the Expansion Office, whose task was to develop and implement the plan to consolidate the campuses to Glenside. (Author's collection.)

According to the December 1962 *Bulletin of Beaver College*, "The college community is enjoying life as a 'one-campus college' for the first time in thirty-four years. President Edward D. Gates has pointed out that this first year will be a period of transition and that a number of adjustments will be made in our program. Changes and new customs are the new fashion for the 1962–63 year." Seen here is a sketch of the proposed campus. (Arcadia University Archives.)

DORMITORIES, DINING HALL AND STUDENT UNION

"The new air-conditioned $600,000 [$6,073,331 in 2024] library with space for 100,000 books. Three new dormitories costing a total of $2,210,000 [$22,370,102 in 2024] and accommodating four hundred students. The new $650,000 [$6,579,422 in 2024] classroom building. A $400,000 [$4,048,887 in 2024] dining hall. A new $85,000 [$860,388 in 2024] health center," noted the December 1962 *Bulletin of Beaver College*. Seen here is a sketch of the proposed campus. (Arcadia University Archives.)

The Eugenia Fuller Atwood Library was built in 1962 as part of the campus consolidation project. Pictured here are Eugenia Fuller Atwood, benefactor and vice president of the board of trustees from 1960 to 1966, and her husband, John C. Atwood Jr., at the cornerstone dedication on April 29, 1962. Today, within the Landman Library, the Atwood Circulating Collection honors Eugenia Fuller Atwood. (Arcadia University Archives.)

"The Heart Of The College . . . The beautiful three-story Eugenia Fuller Atwood Library named in honor of Eugenia Fuller Atwood (May 13, 1895–September 1985) of Chestnut Hill, Pa. Vice President of the Board of Trustees. This photograph combines the new and the old with Grey Towers to the right in the background." This caption and image are from the December 1962 *Bulletin of Beaver College.* (Arcadia University Archives.)

Also in the *Bulletin of Beaver College*, "In Concert . . . The classroom building (right) and side view of the Eugenia Fuller Atwood Library (left). The three-story classroom building contains lecture and seminar rooms, the visual aids and language laboratories, faculty and academic offices." Its basement was a designated fallout shelter during the 1960s. In 1995, it was renamed after Pres. Riley T. Taylor, who served from 1859 to 1894. (Arcadia University Archives.)

Included in the *Bulletin of Beaver College* was "Blending Harmoniously . . . Are the three new three-story dormitory units with accommodations for a total of four hundred. The capacity of this dormitory [Kistler Hall] is 142 students." Note the castle's turrets, which are visible behind and above the dorm's roof line. (Arcadia University Archives.)

"Comfortable Lounges . . . Students relax in the main lounges of the new dormitories which also are used for informal entertainment. The lounges are stone and walnut paneled with a massive woodburning fireplace. Through the trustees, a dedicated faculty and staff, and many other loyal supporters—alumnae, church men and women, and of the friends—today Beaver has one of the most modern college campuses in the country," as published in the *Bulletin of Beaver College*, December 1962. (Arcadia University Archives.)

The *Bulletin of Beaver College* also published the following: "Spacious . . . Is the word for the two-story dining hall building. This structure contains a dining room for the resident students, a private dining area, kitchens, dietitian's office, a Chatterbox, faculty and dining room, and bookstore." Floor-to-ceiling glass panels were advertised as taking full advantage of the natural light and presenting a beautiful view of the campus. (Arcadia University Archives.)

Prof. Benton Murdoch Spruance (June 25, 1904–December 6, 1967) began his career at Beaver College in 1926 as a part-time instructor teaching interior decoration while still a student at the Pennsylvania Academy of the Fine Arts. Spruance was the chair of the arts department at Beaver College from 1933 to 1967 as well as chairman of the printmaking department of the Philadelphia College of Art. (Arcadia University Archives.)

The most notable feature of the Benton Spruance Art Center (originally Brookside Hall, renamed in 1969) is its large smokestack, which was part of the former powerhouse. The surrounding ground also housed the Little Theater (constructed in 1966) as well as an art studio and painting classrooms. *Dr. Faustus Lights the Lights* was the first production in the Little Theater on November 15, 1966. (Arcadia University Archives.)

Pictured here in 1966, from left to right, are an unnamed craftsman, Judith Elder (theater department), Benton Spruance (fine arts department), and Charles Hall (religion department) discussing the plans for the Little Theater while under construction. (Arcadia University Archives.)

In 1962, George Ruck gifted Beaver College $85,000 ($860,388 in 2024) to build the Ruck Health Center. This circular building mimicked the shape of the castle turrets. The name was changed to the George Ruck Faculty Suite when the larger Health Sciences Center addition was opened in 1994. (Arcadia University Archives.)

This photograph from 1962 shows Kistler Hall (Dorm A) and Dilworth Hall (Dorm B) under construction. Thomas Hall, completed in 1956, sits between the two construction sites. Tunnels and hallways connect these three dorms to one another and to the dining hall and the Chat. (Arcadia University Archives.)

This 1962 image shows the dining hall under construction. Later, much of this glass facade would be covered with cinder block when the entire building was expanded in 1996–1997. Today, the dining hall is still located on the second level, while the lower level houses the campus bookstore, meeting areas, the Black Box Theater, and the Arcadia radio station. (Arcadia University Archives.)

On May 18, 1963, the dedication ceremony of Kistler Hall, formerly known as Dorm A, took place. A portrait of Dr. Raymon Kistler, honorary president, was unveiled by members of the class of 1938 as part of their 25th reunion gift. Pictured from left to right are Barbara (Fleck) Stitzinger, class of 1938; Dr. Raymon Kistler, honorary president of Beaver College; Clara Agnes (Taylor) Harveson, class of 1938; and Dr. Ira Kraybill, member of the board of trustees. (Arcadia University Archives.)

In 1967, the dorm built in 1962 formerly known as Dorm B was renamed in honor of Reba R. Dilworth of Wynnewood and her late husband, Walter H. Dilworth, devoted friends of the college. Walter served on the college's board of trustees from 1956 until his death in 1961. (Arcadia University Archives.)

In 1967, the dorm built in 1962 formerly known as Dorm C was renamed in honor of Vira Heinz (1888–1983) of Pittsburgh, a member of the board of trustees (1937–1967) and secretary of the board of trustees (1947–1967), in recognition of her distinguished service to the college. Vira married Clifford Heinz, son of Henry Heinz, founder of the food processing company. The North Annex addition was constructed in the early 1970s. (Arcadia University Archives.)

Seen at left is The Villa, originally a house built around 1920. It was used by Beaver as a dorm from 1963 until the early 1970s. Still standing today, it is located at 430 Limekiln Pike. The Villa housed about two dozen students and had its own student ecosystem due to its 10-minute walking distance from the campus. Another off-campus living accommodation, 777 Limekiln Pike, was provided by Beaver at the time. (Arcadia University Archives)

The science academic building cost $3.5 million at the time of construction ($29,280,000 in 2024). The three-story, L-shaped concrete building was designed by Geddes Brecher Qualls Cunningham, an architectural firm in Philadelphia and Princeton, New Jersey. Ground-breaking ceremonies were held on March 20, 1969. It was named the Marion Angell Boyer Hall of Science and was completed in January 1971. Featured in the building is the John V. Calhoun Amphitheatre studio and theater. (Arcadia University Archives)

Grey Towers, well loved by the students, alumni, and staff of the university, was officially designated a national historic landmark on October 11, 1985. Pictured from left to right are Susan Smyth Armizer, class of 1959; acting president Bette Landman; Marilyn Cranin, class of 1954; and Betsy Landquist, class of 1954. The plaque pictured now sits prominently on the left side of the castle's entrance. This image is from the October 16, 1985, issue of the *Beaver News*. (Arcadia University Archives)

The Catherine M. and Harry G. Kuch Recreation and Athletic Center opened in January 1993. In 2010–2012, the University Commons student center was built as an addition to the front of the Kuch Recreation and Athletic Center facing Haber Green (formerly Kuch Field). Pictured is the Kuch building before the 2010–2012 addition was constructed. (Arcadia University Archives.)

Knight Hall, pictured here, opened in January 1997. The four-story building houses seven- and five-person suites, with a capacity of 120 students, as well as lower levels that house academic and administrative offices. The university began housing students in apartment-style housing in September 2001. (Arcadia University Archives.)

Larsen Hall, located at 1601 Church Road, is home to the College of Global Studies (TCGS). In 2009, the building was named in honor of David C. Larsen, executive director of TCGS and a vice president of the university from 1988 to 2008. The structure, built in 1904, originally powered the Philadelphia Rapid Transit trolleys that ran from Glenside to Willow Grove Park. It was acquired by the university in 2000. (Arcadia University Archives.)

The lawn area in the center of the Glenside Campus, pictured here, once had quite a slope to it. The lawn (Haber Green), now level, is named after alumna Lois Haber, class of 1971, and her husband, Michael. Lois holds the distinction of becoming the first alumna ever appointed chair of the university's board of trustees. In 2011, she dedicated Haber Green to the class of 1971. This image appeared in the 1971 Beaver College yearbook. (Arcadia University Archives.)

In 2013, a student lost control of their car and struck Murphy Bridge. The entire right side of the bridge, with its two elevated urns, was heavily damaged. The damaged urns were salvaged and repaired. However, given their age and condition, it was determined that they should not return to the bridge location due to vibration. Instead, they were placed on the ground at the bridge approaches. This photograph is from the 1960 Beaver College yearbook. (Arcadia University Archives.)

Guests of the Harrisons would enter the estate through the Gatehouse Arch. After Beaver College purchased the estate, the gatehouse was briefly used as student housing. Students knew this building as the French House and the Lodge (named after Glenn Lodge in 1936). In 1957, it was designated a music conservatory known as Blake Hall after being remodeled by Mr. and Mrs. John Blake in memory of their daughter, Virginia Carson Blake. (Arcadia University Archives.)

Blake Hall was renamed Blankley Alumni House in recognition of alumna Rosemary Deniken Blankley, class of 1957, in 2005. Blankley played varsity field hockey, basketball, and lacrosse while at Beaver. She represented her country, playing on the US hockey team in 1955 and 1956. In 2007, she became a lifetime trustee, having served on the board of trustees since 1993. In 2023, the building was renamed the Alumni House at Blankley Hall. (Author's collection.)

Today known as the Alumni Fund Walk of Pride (dedicated on November 15, 1997), this lane, pictured in the 1930s, led guests of the Harrison family from the gatehouse up to the castle. It later became a thoroughfare for students to drive and park their cars along. In this picture, all that is present is the lane and the wishing well. Today, the dining hall is located on the left, and Heinz Hall is located on the right. (Arcadia University Archives.)

In November 2019, the Arcadia Gateway Arch on Easton Road was closed to pedestrian traffic, and a new, temporary entrance was established north of the arch. Facilities Management began an evaluation of the impact of moisture intrusion and vibration from the adjacent roadway on the stability of the arch, which had begun to lean onto Easton Road. (Arcadia University Archives.)

To ensure the safety of the campus community, as well as passing motorists, the arch was taken down. Each stone and limestone decorative element was laser scanned and cataloged to create a map of the arch. In addition, all elements were carefully and individually removed—stone by stone—cleaned, and stored in a sequential order at a secure location. Plans are to reinstall the arch at a later date. (Author's collection.)

Four

Beaver College and Arcadia University

Life on Campus through the Years

Through university yearbooks and self-published newspaper archives, the remainder of this book will look back at more carefree times in our lives. The name of the newspaper at Beaver College/Arcadia University has changed over the years: the *College Messenger*, the *Periscope* (1925–1926), *Campus Crier* (1926–1930), the *Beaver News* (1935–1986), and the *Tower* (1987–2013). The name of the yearbook at Beaver College/Arcadia University has also changed over the years: the *Beechbark* (1927–1935), the *Beaver Log* (1937–1942), the *Log of Beaver College* (1943–2001), and *Arcadia University Enthymion* (2001–present). These publications document daily activities of campus life including the many clubs and athletic teams that students could partake in. For years, Beaver/Arcadia students have excelled in intercollegiate competitions by engaging in (field) hockey, basketball, softball, golf, lacrosse, track, tennis, swimming, and riflery, to name a few. Early rivals were Bryn Mawr, Ursinus, Swarthmore, Drexel, New York University, University of Pennsylvania, Temple University, and William and Mary. Students could join Glee Club, Theater Playhouse, and the Student Government Association or clubs that organized events such as May Day, prom, and the song contest. The following societies had a presence in the past at Beaver College: Lambda Delta Alpha, Pi Delta Epsilon, Psi Chi, Alpha Kappa Alpha, and Pentathlon.

Pictured in the 1928 Beaver College yearbook is the varsity hockey team: "In the first snowstorm of the season Beaver was defeated by Rosemont 2-1, after a hard fight on Rosemont's field. The playing back and forth kept the game at an exciting pitch until the end when all were glad to share the warmth and hospitality of the open fire and tea before leaving for home." (Arcadia University Archives.)

A sacred senior tradition at Beaver College was the Lantern Parade. All the seniors wore white dresses and carried illuminated Japanese lanterns. The seniors then sang a farewell song while giving their place to their successors, the present juniors. This impressive ceremony was usually held at twilight, lending enchantment and atmosphere to an almost sad but fond farewell. This image is from the 1930 Beaver College yearbook. (Arcadia University Archives.)

According to the 1929 Beaver College yearbook, "The splendors of the May Queen and her attractive attendants were glorified by the brightest of suns, illuminating the surroundings, causing the trees, the grass, the very towers of our great magnificent castle. . . . Those who took part were proud and happy to be associated with such a successful event; and those who looked on were extremely fortunate to have seen in reality such a scene as the first activity held on the grounds of Grey Towers." This May Day celebration took place on May 10, 1929. (Arcadia University Archives.)

Carolyn Mulholland
May Queen

Helen Wenger
Maid of Honor

The popular song contest tradition started in 1932. It took place the evening before the Thanksgiving holiday. The show played to a standing-room-only audience consisting of the entire college community and many alumnae. In this image from the 1953 Beaver College yearbook, "the Jolly Juniors" (class of 1954) were victorious as they shouted the news of Beaver's sale and the move to the new campus. (Arcadia University Archives.)

Interest in the song contest tradition faded in the late 1960s due to changing times. As fewer and fewer students participated, it was discontinued in 1968. Pictured here from the 1968 Beaver College yearbook is the class of 1970 performing at the last song contest event. (Arcadia University Archives.)

The graduation procession heads to Murphy Hall. A message on the back of the photograph states, "Beaver College holds 79th commencement. Member of the class of eighty-two graduates of Beaver College at Jenkintown PA., enter Murphy Hall for the College's 79th Annual commencement June 14, 1933." (Author's collection.)

A note on the backside of the image says, "Coeds decked in picturesque costumes rehearse the Persian Tableau, which will be one of the features of the Beaver College, annual May Day festival to be held May 12th. Left to right are Helen Lucile Becker, Ruth Shepherd Mitchell, Doris Freihofer, Virginia Sackett, Mary Clark Mattocks, Lillian L. Smith, and Mary Baylor Reinhart. 5/10/1934." (Author's collection.)

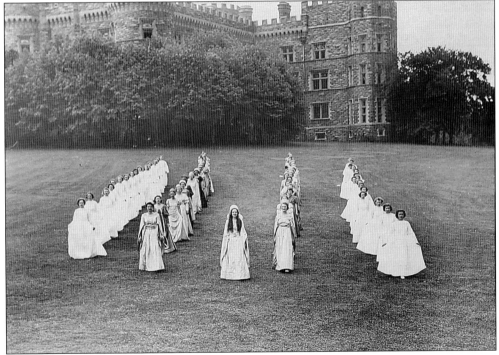

May Day celebrations were first mentioned in the *College Messenger* in June 1884. Written on the back of the photograph is "Beaver students rehearse May Day festival depicting a Scandinavian Fantasy. Students of Beaver College, Jenkintown, PA. Prepare in costume to mark their annual May Day Festival. Here is a general view of the Queen and her Court. 5/14/1937." (Author's collection.)

The Chatterbox opened in 1933 on the Jenkintown Campus. As advertised in the *Beaver News* on September 24, 1943, "Work in the Chatterbox the Beaver student's lifeline is also worthy of praise girls work on the average eight hours week serving ice cream making sandwiches pouring coffee and washing dishes. Thirty-five cents an hour is the reward plus the expressions of gratitude and appreciation of the students and the faculty." (Author's collection.)

The article goes on: "The Chatterbox is the student's place for relaxation. It can be kept such a place if everyone assumes the responsibility of seeing that the dirty dishes are put in the right place on table near the Chatterbox door. For a job in the Chatterbox, see Miss Alden." (Author's collection.)

According to the October 13, 1939, *Beaver News*, "A new coke bar (Chatterbox) in Grey Towers was a pleasant surprise to upperclassmen returning September 1939." The soda fountain was located just off the dining room of Grey Towers, in what was formerly known as the "studio." A new Crosley radio was also provided. There was mention that the floor would be waxed to make dancing possible. (Author's collection.)

Later, the Chatterbox name was shortened to "the Chat," and it was located below the dining hall on the Glenside Campus (pictured here). In 2010, the Chat was relocated to the main level of the newly built Commons area of the Kuch Recreation and Athletic Center. (Arcadia University Archives.)

The Beaver College rifle team formed during the 1935–1936 academic year, with its first match taking place on January 7, 1937. From 1939 to 1951, the rifle team finished among the top teams. In 1948, with Linford Schober as coach, the team won its first national championship. In 1950 and again in 1951, the team repeated its stellar performance, winning the National Women's Intercollegiate Championship. In 2009, the 1948, 1950, and 1951 national champion rifle teams were inducted into Arcadia University Athletic Hall of Fame. This image is from the 1951 Beaver College yearbook. (Arcadia University Archives.)

The rifle range was first located in the Murphy Hall Gymnasium on the Glenside Campus and later in the basement of Huntington Hall on the Jenkintown Campus. Pictured in 1951 are, from left to right, coach Linford D. Schober (1894–1964), Jo Ann Lissfelt, Beverly Gifford, and Ann Little. (Special Collections Research Center, Temple University Libraries.)

Located in the courtyard of Murphy Hall is a plaque that states, "This plaque, presented by the class of 1933, is given to perpetuate the honor to the Junior with the highest academic standing who is chosen to plant the ivy during the annual Class Day Exercises" during senior week. This tradition ended in 1967. Prior to the campus consolidation, the plaque resided at the entrance of the chapel at Taylor Hall on the Jenkintown Campus. (Author's collection.)

Freshman beanies, or dinks, were worn by first-year students from the early 1930s until 1977. Hazing and pranking were not allowed after 1958. The September 15, 1978, *Beaver News* announced that freshmen would no longer be wearing dinks. Pictured are some 1976 first-year students donning their dinks in the halls. (Arcadia University Archives.)

BAILEY, BANKS & BIDDLE CO.
Jewelers Silversmiths Stationers

ESTABLISHED 1832

1218-22 Chestnut Street
PHILADELPHIA

Patented

Makers of the Beaver College Rings
1929 — 1930

SCHOOL RINGS, EMBLEMS
AND TROPHIES
Of the Better Kind

The history of the Beaver College class ring began in 1930. Each May, during a "Ring Breakfast," members of the junior class eagerly accepted their college class rings from a departing senior of their choice. Class rings were symbols of their achievement and were worn with pride. In 1953, the inside of the ring was engraved with the word "Centennial" to mark the 100th anniversary of the institution. This image is from the 1930 Beaver College yearbook. (Arcadia University Archives.)

110

The stone was sardonyx with the Goddess of Wisdom engraved on it. Around the face, "Beaver College" was inscribed in gold. Engraved on the left side was a view of Beaver Hall and the date of the founding of the college (1853). The right side was engraved with a view of Grey Towers and the year of graduation. Ivy leaves, signifying strength, appeared on both sides of the band. (Author's collection.)

Students could purchase and earn brooches, pins, charms, pendants, keys, and fobs by joining and partaking in clubs and organizations on campus. These were popular accessories during the 1930s through the late 1950s. Prior to Beaver College's move to Jenkintown in 1925, rules actually forbade students from wearing any jewelry. (Author's collection.)

Bus transportation (Beaver buses) between the Glenside and Jenkintown Campuses (which took 15 minutes) was a vital part of college life from 1929 to 1962. At first, these buses were painted grey and trimmed in red. With the passing of rules concerning transportation in connection with private schools in the mid-1930s, Beaver buses were painted an eye-catching orange boasting the name "Beaver College" in black letters. Pictured here is the Beaver bus from the 1937–1938 school year. (Arcadia University Archives.)

The April 12, 1946, edition of the *Beaver News* mentions this much-loved transportation: "Contributing to the importance of these vehicles are Beaver's bus drivers without whom the students would feel lost. It is one of them behind the wheel who so thoughtfully holds the bus for a tardy student and who deposits the day students right at the steps of the train station." This image is from the 1960 Beaver College yearbook. (Arcadia University Archives.)

Pictured here is the Dormitory Council for the 1947–1948 school year. The purpose of the Dormitory Council was to be directly responsible for dormitory life, to keep the dormitories orderly, quiet, and attractive, and to be responsible for the general decorum of the students on campus. The council met weekly and at that time reviewed cases of those who had been reported for violation of dormitory rules. This image is from the 1948 Beaver College yearbook. (Arcadia University Archives.)

Jane Louise Morris, class of 1949, represented Beaver College as a contestant in the eighth National Intercollegiate Flying Club Air Meet, which was held at the University of Michigan from May 30 through June 1, 1947. Two hundred people and 50 planes were expected to participate in the event, which was run from the east side of the university's Willow Run Airport. This image is from the *Beaver News* published on May 16, 1947. (Arcadia University Archives.)

In June 1948, seventeen students headed to Europe via boat for 10 weeks to see the first-hand economic effects of World War II and the postwar efforts to rebuild. The success of that summer study initiative spawned several more programs in other disciplines. For the next several summers, both Beaver College students and those invited from neighboring institutions took part in Beaver's European study tours. (Arcadia University Archives.)

In 1965, the Center for Education Abroad was established to enable American undergraduates to study for credit in fully integrated programs in Great Britain, Austria, and elsewhere. In 2009, the Arcadia University Center for Education Abroad transformed into the College of Global Studies at Arcadia University as part of a total restructuring of the university's academic affairs. Students pose at the Palace of Versailles in France in 1948. (Arcadia University Archives.)

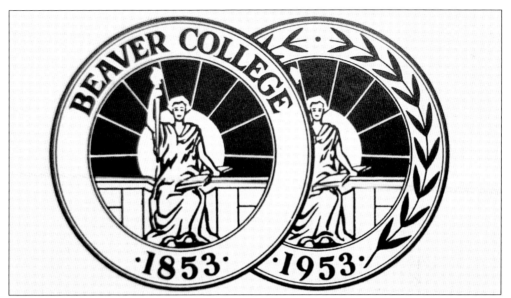

In 1953, Beaver College celebrated its centennial anniversary. The class of 1953 was called the "Centennial Class." Seen here is the special logo the college used for the year on all official correspondence. The year's reunion festivities, which took place on June 6 and 7, had class representatives from all years from 1894 through 1953. This image is from the 1953 Beaver College yearbook. (Arcadia University Archives.)

This photograph was taken on January 8, 1953, at the kick-off of the centennial anniversary events for the year. From left to right are Dr. Raymon Kistler, president of the college; Miriam Becker, class of 1957; Centennial Queen Jacqueline Churchill Strohauer, class of 1953, who cut the anniversary cake; and unidentified. Special events such as receptions, dances, lectures, and concerts took place during the year to commemorate the centennial. (Arcadia University Archives.)

One of the many jobs that was available on campus to students was as an operator on the school's phone switchboard. The switchboard was located just inside the entrance to the castle (where the elevator is located today). This image appeared in the 1965 Beaver College yearbook. (Arcadia University Archives.)

According to the *Beaver News* on November 12, 1968, "17 October 1968 a day which began as so many others, seemingly just another day in the life of the Beaver girl, but, as it progressed a day to be remembered. On that fateful Thursday, the co-curricular policy committee took the big step and plunged into an area of contention to finally affirm the sanctioning of the Association of Beaver College Blacks." This picture is from a recruitment event. (Arcadia University Archives.)

Members of the *Log* meet for their yearbook group photograph in the Classroom Building's fallout shelter. The shelter could hold 100 people and was filled with water, crackers, and other survival instruments. Other buildings on the campus housed similar shelters. This image appeared in the 1968 Beaver College yearbook. (Arcadia University Archives.)

In this 1971 Beaver College yearbook photograph, students wait for classes in the Classroom Building/ Taylor Hall hallway. Very few who attended will ever forget the black and white checkerboard pattern in the tiled flooring of the hallways. (Arcadia University Archives.)

The mail room, then located on the bottom floor of Heinz Hall, as seen in this 1972 Beaver College yearbook image, was very important for students in maintaining their connection to the outside world prior to the internet, email, social media, and cell phones. (Arcadia University Archives.)

Students and alumni took part in telethons to raise funds throughout the years. Known as "phonies," students and alumni would call alumni and others to spread the word. Pictured here is a telethon from the spring of 1972. (Arcadia University Archives.)

OLLEGE TO ADMIT
EN AT ALL LEVELS
SEPTEMBER '73

er College, will admit men s at all levels beginning in ber, 1973, John R. Bunting, an of the Beaver College of trustees, announced last y. The effective date for mission of men to Beaver at a meeting of the board stees held on Tuesday, 6.

aking the announcement nting said, "Beaver College vays been dedicated to a ng reevaluation of the f the college program in at of changing patterns of We believe that Beaver st serve higher education community today as a co-nal institution.

decision has been made g a three-year study and of the question of co-n by the trustees together he faculty, students , ad-tors and alumnae.

of the interesting findings ly revealed was the dearth ll private, coed colleges near the urban centers of tern seaboard. We feel that ning its doors to men, will offer a broader ser-those interested in obtain-ollege education and, par-y, in the kind of academic n provided by the college. es to a survey on coedu-sent to alumnae, faculty dents show that a major-r this move."

r will remain a relatively ollege. At present the en-

rollment is about 1000, including some 250 students from other colleges and universities enrolled in Beaver's International Studies Programs in Great Britain, Vienna and Hong Kong. Men will be admitted as resident, commuting and transfer students. They will be housed in one of the existing resident halls on campus and facilities will be available for the commuting students. The college expects to eventually reach an enrollment of 1200 to 1500 students.

The college officials believe that the curriculum is equally challenging and attractive to both sexes. Among the programs expected to be of special interest to men are the natural sciences, psychology, sociology and fine arts, as well as preparation for teaching and for professional and/or graduate schools. The field work, apprenticeship and internship opportunities add another dimension to the academic program.

Historically Beaver has welcomed men as undergraduates—1860 and again in 1872 when it was chartered as a college "for the education of both sexes." In 1907 another charter change was made limiting the enrollment to women. In recent years Beaver has enrolled a number of men both as special students on campus and in the college's International Programs. This action by the board of trustees implements the 1972 charter change which again permits the college to admit men as degree candidates.

Obituary
Beaver College

by Bonnie Bergman

Suddenly, on the evening of March 5, 1973, Beaver College, a four-year liberal arts school for women, was put to death by the action of some thirty assailants. The action, evidently, was a premeditated one.

The ceaseless rain and the melancholy fog which enveloped the campus, seemed to echo the sadness of the evening.

The college, founded in 1853 in Beaver, Pennsylvania, moved first to Jenkintown and then to the town of Glenside — the site chosen to be its final resting place.

"One hundred and thirty-five years ago the first women were admitted to an American institution of higher learning. Since that time we have become increasingly aware of women's need for higher education and of society's need for educated women. As a college for women, Beaver "was" concerned primarily with the individual student and her unique potential . . . and for her education of her status as a woman . . . women's education requires special attention." For one hundred and twenty years Beaver has dedicated herself to providing a high quality education for women. Now it has ended.

The murder of Beaver College is a deep and senseless loss — one which could have been prevented. The as yet unfathomed consequences of her passing will be realized in the forthcoming years.

In 1973, Beaver College went coed. This was due in large part to Title IX of the Education Amendments of 1972, which prohibited sex (including pregnancy, sexual orientation, and gender identity) discrimination in any education program or activity receiving federal financial assistance. Seen here is how the information was presented to the student body. The update to the college's charter at this time also severed ties with the United Presbyterian Church. Not all felt that this change to go coed was a good idea for future existence. Some felt it would be the end of Beaver College. Although this was a major change, it was far from the death of the institution. This image is from the *Beaver News* issue of March 13, 1973. (Arcadia University Archives.)

Today covered by shrubs, this front corner of the Marion Angell Boyer Hall of Science was at one time used as a corner stage for entertainment and events. Directly inside from this corner is the John V. Calhoun Amphitheatre studio and theater. (Arcadia University Archives.)

Pictured here is the interior of the John V. Calhoun Amphitheatre, located in Boyer Hall on the first floor. It has a seating capacity of 120 people. Boyer also houses classrooms for the biology, chemistry and physics, forensic science, computer science, mathematics, and psychology departments. Its facilities also include computer labs, a greenhouse, and an observatory. (Arcadia University Archives.)

Students spend time together parked outside Thomas and Kistler Halls on what today is the Alumni Fund Walk of Pride. Prior to the Walk of Pride being dedicated, this lane was available to automobile traffic with parking along the side. This image first appeared in the 1979 Beaver College yearbook. (Arcadia University Archives.)

In 1978, instead of electing a homecoming queen, each hall sponsored a guy for homecoming king. Hence the Mr. Beaver Contest was born. In the years following, the Student Programming Board built it into an event of its own, with each year outdoing the previous. Contestants were judged in categories such as swimwear/toga wear, talent, formal, and other questionable categories. This image is from the 1979 Beaver College yearbook. (Arcadia University Archives.)

Woodstock started in 1980. The May 1, 1981, edition of the *Beaver News* stated, "In response to the celebrated success of last year's event, the Day Student Club, Beaver College NORML, and the Student Program Board will be presenting the 2nd Annual Woodstock this Saturday. The event will feature The Sharks (punk), The John-Paul Kat Band (rock 'n roll), and the Trees (new wave) who appeared last year." This photograph appeared in the 1981 Beaver College yearbook. (Arcadia University Archives.)

The first official radio broadcast of WBVR 640 AM (later 630) was on February 16, 1988. The radio station was located in the basement of Dilworth Hall. The station's DJs (students) were permitted to choose their own format. Many DJs played their own albums/tapes, since the station did not have a budget for albums/tapes. Pictured is Jonathan Marley, class of 1989, a DJ at WBVR, as he prepared for his show. This image appeared in the *Tower* on February 18, 1988. (Arcadia University Archives.)

Living arrangements on the upper floors of the castle were only open to senior females prior to 1991. In 1991, the castle's residential demographics changed when senior males were also permitted to reside there. Later, in 2005, changes were again made to the castle's residency eligibility when both first-year females and males were able to live in the historic structure. Pictured is a castle dorm room from the 1972 Beaver College yearbook. (Arcadia University Archives.)

The Black Awareness Society was originally formed in 1968 under the title of the Association of Beaver College Blacks. The intention of the club was to provide a forum for self-expression while discussing various cultural conflicts being experienced by Black people on campus. Members awakened the faculty and administration to the problems they were faced with. Through the influences of the club, they saw to it these issues were dealt with properly. This image appeared in the 1975 Beaver College yearbook. (Arcadia University Archives.)

In 1985, Dr. Bette E. Landman was appointed president of Beaver College. She was the first female president in the institution's history. Prior roles with the institution are as follows: assistant professor of anthropology, 1971–1976; dean, 1976–1985; vice president of academic affairs, 1980–1985; acting president, 1983 and 1985; and president, 1985–2004. Through her extraordinary vision for the institution and unwavering commitment to access and inclusion, Landman reinvigorated the university, doubling enrollment and leading transformative projects, such as constructing seven new buildings and a nationally recognized study abroad program. She led the community through the historic transition from Beaver College to Arcadia University. The Landman Library (established in 2003) is named in her honor. This portrait of Dr. Bette E. Landman hangs in the Landman Library. (Arcadia University Archives.)

Beaver College began a process of inquiry regarding a new name, first by way of a large opinion survey of alumni, friends, students, faculty, and staff. Then the faculty/staff/alumni/trustee/student committee met throughout the summer of 2000 to identify a potential new name for the institution, one that would capture its present and hoped-for future essence. Pictured here is Dr. Bette E. Landman signing the celebratory banner on the night of the name unveiling. (Arcadia University Archives.)

Several potential names were evaluated in nationwide focus groups. At a surprise midnight event on November 20, 2000, it was officially announced that Beaver College would become Arcadia University. The official change of name and status took place at a formal ceremony on July 16, 2001. Seen here is a multiple exposure of the Philadelphia skyline with the PECO Crown Lights announcing, "Beaver College is now Arcadia University." (Photograph by Edward Savaria Jr., courtesy of Arcadia University Archives.)

BIBLIOGRAPHY

Atlas of Cheltenham, Abington and Springfield Townships, Montgomery County, Penna. Philadelphia: A.H. Mueller & Co., 1897.

Beaver College Handbook, 1929–1930.

Beaver College yearbook, various editions.

Bulletin of Beaver College 27, no. 5 (July 1929).

Bulletin of Beaver College 31, no. 2 (April 1931).

Cameron, Samuel M., Mark P. Curchack, and Michael L. Berger. *From Female Seminary to Comprehensive University: A 150-Year History of Beaver College and Arcadia University.* Glenside, PA: Arcadia University, 2003.

Campus Crier, various editions.

Fraise, Richard J. *History of Beaver County, Pennsylvania: Including Its Early Settlement; Its Erection into a Separate County; Its Subsequent Growth and Development; Sketches of Its Boroughs, Villages, and Townships; Portraits of Some of Its Prominent Men; Biographies of Many of Its Representative Citizens; Statistics, Etc.* Philadelphia and Chicago: A. Warner & Co.: 1888.

Harrison, William Welsh. *Harrison, Waples and Allied Families: Being the Ancestry of George Leib Harrison of Philadelphia and of His Wife Sarah Ann Waples.* Philadelphia: Edward Stern & Co. Inc., 1910.

Hayes, E.L. *Illustrated Atlas of the Upper Ohio River and Valley from Pittsburgh, Pa. to Cincinnati, Ohio: From United States Official and Special Surveys.* Philadelphia: Titus, Simmons & Titus, 1877.

Hexamer, Ernest. Hexamer General Surveys. Vol. 30, Plates 2952–2953. 1896.

Historic American Buildings Survey. Grey Towers, 450 South Easton Road, Beaver College, Glenside, Montgomery County, PA. Pennsylvania Montgomery County Glenside, 1933. Photograph. www.loc.gov/item/pa2988/.

Matthews, Dr. Kenneth D. "Grey Towers Castle Landmark Celebration. October 5–12, 1985." Glenside, PA: Beaver College, 1985.

———. National Register of Historic Places Inventory Nomination Form, 1984. ID 80003578. npgallery.nps.gov.

Property Atlas of Montgomery County, Penna., Volume C, Including the Townships of Abington and Cheltenham and the Boroughs of Jenkintown and Rockledge. Philadelphia: Franklin Survey Company, 1937.

ABOUT THE ORGANIZATION

Arcadia University is a top-ranked private university in Greater Philadelphia that provides an educational experience that is values-based; rooted in justice, equity, diversity, and inclusion (JEDI); and places students at the center. *U.S. News & World Report* ranks Arcadia as the best college in Pennsylvania and among the best in the nation for study abroad, as well as among the most innovative colleges, and the *Princeton Review* has ranked Arcadia among the best in the region for nine straight years. The university's physical therapy and physician assistant programs are nationally ranked in their respective categories by *U.S. News & World Report*. Visit arcadia.edu.

DISCOVER THOUSANDS OF LOCAL HISTORY BOOKS
FEATURING MILLIONS OF VINTAGE IMAGES

Arcadia Publishing, the leading local history publisher in the United States, is committed to making history accessible and meaningful through publishing books that celebrate and preserve the heritage of America's people and places.

Find more books like this at
www.arcadiapublishing.com

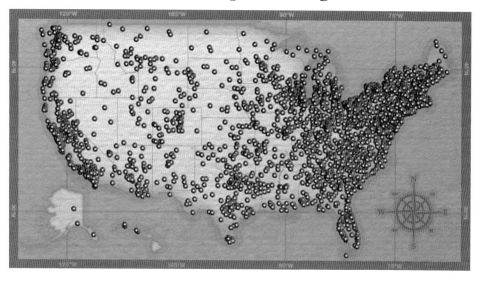

Search for your hometown history, your old stomping grounds, and even your favorite sports team.